TAINTED LOVE:

STAY OR GO?

Navigating Tough Relationship
Decisions in Addiction

ANDREA SEYDEL

Copyright © 2024 by Andrea Seydel

All rights reserved.

Published and Distributed in Canada by Live Life Happy Publishing.
www.livelifehappypublishing.com

All rights reserved. No part of this book may be reproduced by any mechanical, photographic, or electronic process, or in the form of a phonograph recording: Nor may it be stored in a retrieval system, transmitted, or otherwise be copied for public or private use- other than for "fair use" as brief quotations embodied in articles and reviews without prior written permission of the publisher. If you use any of the information in this book for yourself, which is your constitutional right, the author and the publisher assumes no responsibility for your actions.

Library of Congress Cataloging-in-Publication Data

Andrea Seydel

Tainted Love: Stay or Go?

Categories: Health>Addiction & Recovery, Health> Addiction & Recovery> Twelve-Step Programs, Parenting & Relationships › Marriage & Adult Relationships

ISBN E-Book: 978-1-990461-76-7

ISBN Paperback: 978-1-990461-77-4

ISBN Audio: 978-1-990461-78-1

Cover Design: Live Life Happy Publishing

Live Life Happy Publishing

PUBLISHER'S NOTE & AUTHOR DISCLAIMER

This publication is designed to provide accurate and authoritative information concerning the subject matter covered. It is sold to understand that the publisher and author are not engaging in or rendering any psychological, medical or other professional services. If expert assistance or counselling is needed, seek the services of a competent medical professional. For immediate support call your local crisis line. The following book could contain actual events and experiences that the author has encountered in their life. However, some names and specific locations have been changed or omitted to protect the privacy and confidentiality of the individuals involved. The changes do not alter the story's integrity or its messages.

Dedication

For all those who intimately understand the challenges of navigating addiction within a relationship, this book is dedicated to you. Your resilience in the face of adversity is both admirable and inspiring. May this book offer you comfort, guidance, and empowerment as you journey through the complexities of love and addiction.

CONTENTS

Introduction: *A Tough Road* 7
Acknowledging the Complexity of Relationships Affected by Addiction

Chapter 1: *If You Loved Me You'd Stop* 13
Understanding Addiction and Its Impact on Relationships

Chapter 2: *Saving You Is Killing Me* 29
Accessing Your Relationship: Navigating Love Amidst Addiction's Challenges

Chapter 3: *It'll get better. Or will it?* 51
Navigating Love's Toughest Moments: Hope and Reality

Chapter 4: *Bruised Heart* 71
Unmasking Shadows: Recognizing Abuse and Unhealthy Patterns

Chapter 5: *Crossing The Line* 97
Navigating Boundaries, Ultimatums, and Rules for Love

Chapter 6: *With or Without You* 129
Exploring Your Options: Finding Your Path Forward

Chapter 7: *If You Could Read My Mind* 147
Trusting Your Instincts: Finding Clarity

Chapter 8: *Putting My Oxygen Mask On* 173
Affirming Your Value and Empowering Your Path Forward

Conclusion 201

INTRODUCTION

A TOUGH ROAD

Acknowledging the Complexity of Relationships Affected by Addiction

Let's be real – navigating a relationship with someone struggling with addiction is incredibly challenging. It's one of the hardest things you'll ever have to face. There's no simple solution or easy answer. Addiction has a way of transforming the person we love, and suddenly we find ourselves dealing with situations we never could have imagined.

It's a confusing and often overwhelming journey, filled with a mix of empathy for our loved one and the pain of being treated poorly – lies, manipulation, and more. What we once thought we wouldn't tolerate somehow becomes our new reality.

Nobody prepares us for this rollercoaster of emotions and challenges. Deciding the fate of the relationship while navigating the impact of addiction on your own well-being and mental health is unlike any other relationship decision you'll face. Addiction adds a layer of complexity that only those who have experienced it can truly understand.

This book is designed to help you navigate a relationship with someone struggling with addiction. It's a guide through the murky waters of love and addiction, offering insights, support, and a comforting hand to hold along the way.

Feeling torn between staying and going, unsure of what the right choice may be – it's a weighty burden that many of us carry in relationships affected by addiction. On one hand, there's the hope that staying will lead to a better outcome, that somehow things will improve and our loved one will find their way back to us. But on the other hand, there's the fear of enduring more stress, more heartache, and more uncertainty about the future.

And if we entertain the thought of leaving, it's met with its own set of fears and doubts. The fear of being alone, of navigating life's challenges solo, and the sadness of leaving behind someone we care deeply about. There's a whirlwind of emotions – uncertainty, pain, fear – that swirls around us, clouding our judgment and leaving us feeling adrift in a sea of confusion.

But amidst the chaos, my goal with this book is to provide you with a refuge – a warm, inviting space where you can find solace and support. Here, you'll come to understand the intricate dynamics of addiction and its impact on relationships, gaining clarity on how to safeguard your own well-being and mental health.

I want to empower you to embrace self-care, self-compassion, and resilience, regardless of the path you choose. By shedding light on what lies at your deepest core – your needs, your values, your desires – I aim to equip you with the tools you need to protect yourself in the face of addiction.

You're not alone in this journey. Together, we'll navigate the twists and turns, finding strength in our shared experiences and emerging stronger and more resilient on the other side.

A Heart-to-Heart: Sharing My Journey and Why I'm Here to Help You Navigate This Tough Decision

I want to open up and share a piece of my heart with you because I believe it's essential for us to connect on a deeper level. In my own journey, I've walked the painful path of loving someone battling addiction. It's a road filled with uncertainty, emotional turmoil, and heartache that cuts deep.

I know firsthand the internal struggle of deciding whether to stay or go. It's like carrying a heavy burden on your shoulders, wondering if you're doing the right thing, questioning if you're letting them down or sacrificing your own well-being by staying. The truth is, there are no easy answers, and no one can make that decision for you but you.

I've been in that place of uncertainty, grappling with the should I stay or should I leave dilemma. The fear of what might happen if I left haunted me – the thought of him spiraling down a darker path or worse, losing himself to his addiction. I held onto hope, hoping against hope that the person I fell in love with would return, but instead, I was faced with an empty shell of the man he once was.

The lies, the deceit, the broken promises – they became the norm in our relationship, and it broke my heart to see him choose drugs over our love and the life we had planned together. I kept giving chances, setting deadlines, hoping things would get better, but they never did. In the end, he made the choice to leave, leaving me to pick up the pieces of our shattered dreams.

I share my story with you not to dwell on the past but to let you know that you're not alone in this journey. I understand the pain, the confusion, and the overwhelming sense of loss that comes with loving someone battling addiction. And I want you to know that it's okay to feel all of it – the anger, the sadness, the frustration.

There's no judgment here, only compassion and understanding. My background in psychology, particularly positive psychology and resilience, has equipped me with the tools to support you through this difficult time. I've turned my pain into purpose, and I'm here to walk alongside you every step of the way.

I know how difficult it is to balance the feelings of love and compassion with the need to protect your own well-being. It's a delicate dance, and there are no easy answers. But I'm here to tell you that you're not alone. I've been through it, and I'm here to walk alongside you every step of the way.

In this book, I share the journey of loving someone with an addiction – the highs, the lows, and everything in between. I want you to know that whatever you're feeling right now, it's valid. Whether you're struggling to decide whether to stay or go, or you're feeling lost and overwhelmed, I'm here to help.

I wrote this book because I know firsthand how hard it is to navigate a relationship touched by addiction. Traditional relationship advice often falls short in these situations, and that's why I wanted to create a resource specifically for us – those who are facing the unique challenges of loving someone with addiction.

Throughout these pages, we'll explore the complexities of addiction and its impact on relationships. We'll delve into the nuances of love, hope, and reality, and we'll confront the difficult truths that come with loving someone who is struggling.

But most importantly, we'll do it together. I'll be your guide, your confidant, and your friend as we navigate this journey. My background in psychology, particularly positive psychology and resilience, has equipped me with the tools to support you through this difficult time.

Let's Go on a Journey Together: Finding Clarity and Compassion Along The Way

So welcome, my friend, to a journey of self-discovery and healing. I'm here to walk alongside you, offering a guiding hand and a compassionate ear as we navigate the twists and turns of loving someone with addiction. Think of me as your new confidant, your trusted ally, and your unwavering supporter.

Throughout this journey, we'll delve deep into the heart of understanding addiction and how it shapes our relationships. Together, we'll explore the complexities of assessing your relationship amidst the challenges of addiction, facing the harsh realities of love's toughest moments, and embracing the freedom of setting boundaries that honor your well-being.

Our path forward is illuminated by the power of knowledge and insight, guiding us toward clarity and understanding. We'll explore your options with open hearts and minds, trusting our instincts to lead us toward the path that feels right for you. And as we move forward, my goal is to empower you to prioritize your well-being, build resilience, and embrace the strength within you.

No matter where you are on this journey, remember that you are not alone. My hope is that this book serves as a beacon of light in the darkness, offering perspective, strength, and support as you navigate the challenges of loving someone with addiction. Together, let's find the path forward that honors your truth and empowers you to flourish, no matter the obstacles we may face. Are you ready? Let's begin.

CHAPTER 1

IF YOU LOVED ME YOU'D STOP

Understanding Addiction and Its Impact on Relationships

Introduction

If You Loved Me You'd Stop – it's a phrase that echoes through the halls of countless relationships touched by addiction, including mine. Maybe you've found yourself whispering those words in the depths of despair, hoping against hope that your love alone could break through the barriers of addiction and bring your loved one back to you.

But as we dive into Understanding Addiction and Its Impact on Relationships, I've come to realize that addiction doesn't play by the rules of love. It's a force of its own, driven by cravings and compulsions that defy reason and logic.

No matter how much we pour our hearts into loving someone struggling with addiction, it's not enough to magically make them stop. Addiction is a complex beast that requires professional help, support, and sometimes, even a wake-up call from life itself.

Understanding the nature of addiction has taught me that love alone isn't a cure-all. It's a hard pill to swallow, but it's also a freeing realization. It liberates us from the burden of thinking that we somehow failed to love them enough to make them stop.

So, if you've ever felt the weight of those words – If You Loved Me You'd Stop – know that you're not alone. But also know that it's not a reflection of your love or your worth. It's simply a testament to the fierce grip of addiction and the journey we must embark on with empathy, resilience, and self-compassion.

In this chapter, we'll explore the complexities of addiction and its impact on relationships, shedding light on the challenges we face and offering insights to guide us through the storm. Get ready to delve deep into what addiction truly entails and how it shapes our personal connections. We'll unravel the self-centered nature of addiction and explore the common patterns and behaviors that emerge in its wake.

As we navigate through the complexities of addiction, we'll also confront the harsh realities it brings, providing you with a clear understanding of what you're facing. -*In case you weren't already aware of its destructive path. At least you won't feel alone.* Along the way, we'll address the rollercoaster of emotions you're likely experiencing, offering guidance and support to help you navigate this challenging terrain with courage and compassion.

Understanding Addiction: A Realistic Perspective

Have you ever felt like you're constantly juggling your own needs and well-being against the overwhelming demands of your loved one's addiction?

CHAPTER 1: IF YOU LOVED ME YOU'D STOP

Let's get real about what addiction truly looks like and how it affects not only the individual struggling but also the loved ones surrounding them.

Addiction has the power to wreak havoc on relationships, leaving us feeling burned out, stressed, and utterly exhausted. We may find ourselves uncertain about the future of our relationship, questioning whether we can continue to hold it together amidst the chaos. It's not uncommon to feel completely at your wit's end or to grapple with feelings of confusion about the situation at hand. Deep down, we may recognize that there's a problem, even if we're hesitant to acknowledge it fully.

The self-centered nature of addiction can be especially challenging to navigate. As the focus shifts onto the addiction itself, we may find ourselves languishing in the shadows, our own needs and well-being sidelined. Holding onto hope amidst the unpredictability of addiction can feel like an uphill battle, with each day bringing its own set of ups and downs. We may catch glimpses of the person we once knew and loved, only to watch helplessly as addiction takes hold and transforms them into mere shells of their former selves.

Despite the exhaustion and uncertainty, the decision to walk away from or stay in a relationship plagued by addiction is never easy. Years of investment and shared experiences can make the thought of leaving feel overwhelming, even when things are at their worst. We may grapple with conflicting emotions, torn between our desire to salvage the relationship and our own need for self-preservation.

Throughout this journey, it's essential to recognize the toll that addiction takes on ourselves. We find ourselves caught in the line of fire, grappling with the fallout of addiction's relentless grip. But by acknowledging the realities of addiction and its impact on relationships, we can begin to chart a path forward with clarity and resilience.

Understanding the Self-Centered Nature of Addiction: A Closer Look

Have you ever felt like your loved one's addiction takes precedence over everything else in your relationship?

One of the most challenging aspects of being in a relationship with someone struggling with addiction is grappling with the self-centered nature of the condition. Addiction consumes our partner's thoughts, actions, and priorities, leaving little room for anything else. It becomes the sole focus of their existence, overshadowing even the most fundamental aspects of their relationships.

In the throes of addiction, our partner's primary devotion is to the substance or behavior they're addicted to. Nothing else matters as much as satisfying their cravings or feeding their dependency. This single-minded pursuit can lead to neglect and disregard for the needs, feelings, and well-being of their loved ones, including us.

The relentless grip of addiction often manifests in behaviors that are harmful to both the individual and their relationships. Lies, manipulation, deceit, and broken promises become commonplace as our partner prioritizes their addiction above all else. This betrayal of trust and lack of reliability can erode the foundation of even the strongest relationships, leaving us feeling disillusioned, hurt, and abandoned. *To put it softly!*

Being in a relationship with an addict is exceptionally challenging because it feels like we're constantly competing for their attention and affection with something that holds such a powerful sway over them. Despite our best efforts to provide love, support, and understanding, we often find ourselves playing second fiddle to their addiction.

Not to mention, addiction thrives in secrecy and isolation, further straining our relationship dynamics. Our partner may withdraw emotionally or physically, leaving us feeling disconnected and alone in our struggles. This sense of isolation can exacerbate feelings of resentment, frustration, and helplessness, making it even harder to maintain a healthy and fulfilling relationship.

In essence, the self-centered nature of addiction makes it incredibly difficult to sustain a strong and stable relationship. The constant battle for our partner's attention and affection, coupled with the betrayal and hurt caused by their addictive behaviors, can take a significant toll on our emotional well-being. Despite our love and commitment, navigating a relationship with an addict often feels like an uphill battle against an insurmountable force.

Do you find yourself constantly competing for your loved one's attention and affection against their addiction?

The Self-Centered Nature of Addiction: Overcoming Its Impact on Relationships

Addiction often manifests as a self-centered pursuit, consuming thoughts, behaviors, and actions in the relentless quest for the addictive substance or behavior. This self-absorption can strain relationships and leave loved ones feeling neglected, emotionally drained, and overwhelmed. Let's delve into why addiction breeds self-centeredness and how prioritizing one's well-being is crucial in navigating its impact on relationships.

Addiction's Self-Centeredness: Understanding the Dynamics

Preoccupation: Addiction monopolizes the individual's thoughts, leaving little room to consider the needs and concerns of others as they obsess over obtaining and using the substance.

Loss of Perspective: The pursuit of addiction distorts priorities and values, overshadowing relationships, responsibilities, and personal well-being, often making addicts oblivious to the harm they cause.

Manipulation and Deception: Addicts may resort to deceitful tactics to sustain their addiction, eroding trust and straining relationships as they prioritize their cravings over honesty and integrity.

Neglecting Responsibilities: Obligations and commitments take a backseat to addiction, leaving loved ones feeling overlooked and unimportant in the face of the addict's relentless pursuit of their next fix.

Impacts on Relationships: A Closer Look

Emotional Strain: Loved ones experience emotional turmoil as they grapple with feelings of neglect, frustration, and resentment in the wake of addiction's self-centeredness.

Codependency: The self-absorbed behavior of addicts often fosters codependent relationships, where loved ones enable the addiction by prioritizing the addict's needs above their own.

Financial Burden: Addiction's financial toll can strain relationships, creating instability and resentment as loved ones bear the brunt of the addict's self-centered spending habits.

Trust Issues: Manipulative behavior breeds mistrust, making it difficult for loved ones to believe the addict's words or actions, further eroding the foundation of their relationship.

Neglected Needs: The addict's self-absorption leaves loved ones feeling overlooked and unimportant, leading to feelings of loneliness, abandonment, and emotional exhaustion.

Prioritizing Self-Care: A Path to Healing

Recognizing the toll of addiction's self-centeredness, it becomes paramount for loved ones to prioritize their own well-being. By setting boundaries, seeking support, and practicing self-compassion, they can navigate the challenges of addiction with resilience and clarity. More on this in later chapters.

How has delving into addiction's self-centered nature enhanced your understanding of its negative effects on relationships?

Recognizing Patterns: Understanding Behaviors in Relationships Affected by Addiction

In navigating relationships touched by addiction, our instinct to support and care for our loved ones often stems from a place of deep love and cherished memories. However, it can be disheartening to find ourselves labeled as codependent or enablers simply for our acts of kindness and compassion. Instead of viewing these behaviors through a negative lens, let's take a fresh approach to understanding them as the actions of caring, kind-hearted individuals.

Codependency and enabling are terms often associated with relationships affected by addiction, but they carry a weight that fails to capture the complexity of the dynamics at play. From a place of love and compassion, we may find ourselves falling into patterns of codependency, where our sense of self becomes intertwined with the well-being of our loved one. We may go to great lengths to accommodate their needs, prioritize their desires, and shield them from the consequences of their actions, all in an effort to maintain the relationship and alleviate their suffering.

However, this dynamic can quickly become unhealthy for everyone involved. As we pour our energy and resources into supporting our loved ones, we may find ourselves depleted, exhausted, and emotionally drained. Our own needs and well-being often take a backseat as we focus solely on the needs of the addict, leading to feelings of frustration, resentment, and even despair.

It's essential to recognize that while our intentions may be rooted in love, the consequences of codependency and enabling can be detrimental to both ourselves and our loved ones. By acknowledging these patterns and understanding their impact, we can begin to cultivate healthier boundaries, prioritize self-care, and seek support to navigate the complexities of addiction with compassion and resilience.

Examining the Realities of Addiction: An Honest Depiction

Addiction brings with it a host of complexities and challenges that can deeply impact relationships. Understanding the realities of addiction is essential for navigating these difficulties with clarity and resilience. Let's explore some key aspects of addiction's impact on relationships:

Realities of Addiction

Unpredictability:
Addiction often manifests in unpredictable behavior patterns, making it challenging for loved ones to anticipate how the addicted individual will act or react in various situations.

The unpredictability of addiction can create an atmosphere of constant tension and anxiety within the relationship, as loved ones never know what to expect next.

This unpredictability can strain communication, erode trust, and create a sense of instability within the relationship.

Uncertainty:
Living with addiction means living with uncertainty about the future. Loved ones may constantly worry about the well-being of the addicted individual and the stability of the relationship.

The uncertainty surrounding addiction can lead to feelings of fear, anxiety, and helplessness, as loved ones grapple with the unknowns of the situation.

This uncertainty can also extend to other areas of life, such as financial stability, family dynamics, and long-term planning, as addiction disrupts the normal rhythms and routines of daily life.

Emotional Turmoil:
Addiction often brings emotional turmoil into relationships, as individuals struggle to cope with the rollercoaster of emotions associated with addiction.

Loved ones may experience a range of intense emotions, including anger, sadness, frustration, and guilt, as they witness the impact of addiction on their loved one and the relationship.

This emotional turmoil can lead to strained communication, conflicts, and a sense of emotional exhaustion for both the addicted individual and their loved ones.

Isolation and Loneliness:
Addiction can lead to feelings of isolation and loneliness for both the addicted individual and their loved ones.

The shame and stigma associated with addiction may cause individuals to withdraw from social interactions and support networks, leading to increased feelings of isolation and alienation.

Loved ones may also feel isolated as they struggle to connect with the addicted individual amidst the chaos of addiction, leading to a sense of loneliness and disconnection within the relationship.

Financial Strain:
Addiction often comes with significant financial implications, as individuals may prioritize funding their addiction over meeting their financial responsibilities.

Loved ones may bear the brunt of this financial strain, as they may be forced to cover expenses, debts, or legal fees incurred as a result of the addicted individual's behavior.

The financial strain of addiction can create tension, conflict, and resentment within the relationship, as loved ones struggle to navigate the financial challenges associated with addiction.

Impact on Physical Health:
Addiction can take a toll on the physical health of both the addicted individual and their loved ones.

Individuals struggling with addiction may neglect their physical health, leading to issues such as malnutrition, sleep disturbances, and increased susceptibility to illness.

Loved ones may also experience physical health problems as a result of the stress, anxiety, and emotional strain associated with addiction, leading to a deterioration in overall well-being for both parties.

Trust Issues:
Addiction often erodes trust within relationships, as loved ones may feel betrayed by the addicted individual's deceptive or manipulative behavior.

The cycle of lies, broken promises, and betrayal can damage trust and undermine the foundation of the relationship, making it difficult to rebuild trust and establish healthy communication.

Legal Consequences:
Addiction can lead to legal troubles, as individuals may engage in illegal activities to obtain drugs or alcohol or may face legal consequences for their addictive behavior.

Loved ones may also be impacted by legal issues arising from addiction, such as dealing with legal fees, court proceedings, or the consequences of the addicted individual's actions.

Impact on Children and Family Dynamics:
Addiction can have profound effects on children and family dynamics, as they may be exposed to the chaos, unpredictability, and emotional turmoil associated with addiction.

Children of addicted individuals may experience neglect, abuse, or trauma, which can have long-term consequences on their emotional and psychological well-being.

Family dynamics may become strained as members struggle to cope with the challenges of addiction, leading to conflicts, resentment, and a breakdown in communication within the family unit.

Relapse and Recovery:
Relapse is a common reality of addiction, as individuals may struggle to maintain sobriety despite their best efforts.

The cycle of relapse and recovery can be emotionally exhausting for both the addicted individual and their loved ones, as they navigate the ups and downs of the recovery journey.

While recovery is possible, it requires ongoing commitment, support, and resilience from all parties involved, as they work together to overcome the challenges of addiction and rebuild their lives.

How do these honest depictions of addiction's realities resonate with your own experiences or observations, and what steps can you take to support yourself in light of these challenges?

Examining the realities of addiction provides us with an honest depiction of the complexities and challenges inherent in relationships affected by addiction. From the unpredictability and uncertainty to the emotional strain and self-centered behaviors, these realities shed light on the multifaceted nature of addiction's impact. By acknowledging these realities, we can begin to navigate our experiences with greater understanding and compassion. Moving forward, it's essential to prioritize self-care, set healthy boundaries, and seek support when needed, empowering ourselves to navigate the journey of loving someone struggling with addiction with resilience and courage

Navigating Emotions: Addressing the Rollercoaster of Feelings in Loving Someone with Addiction

If you're on this journey of loving someone struggling with addiction, you're likely experiencing a whirlwind of emotions right now. It's perfectly normal to feel overwhelmed, frustrated, and even hopeless at times. You might feel like your heart has been through the wringer, but despite the challenges, it's crucial to remember that you're not damaged beyond repair.

Empathy is being tested on every front, as you're faced with the harsh realities of addiction day in and day out. It's understandable to question your own emotions, wondering if you're doing enough, or if you're simply not strong enough to handle the situation. But rest assured, all these emotions are not only valid but also a testament to your humanity and capacity to love deeply.

Feeling anger, sadness, or even resentment towards the person you care about is not a reflection of your character; rather, it's a natural response to the turmoil and chaos that addiction brings into your life. It's okay to feel overwhelmed by the weight of it all, to feel like you're barely keeping your head above water.

You might find yourself questioning why you're still holding on, despite the pain and heartache. It's essential to recognize that your love and dedication are not weaknesses but strengths. They speak to the depth of your compassion and the resilience of your spirit.

In moments of doubt or despair, remember that you're not alone in this journey. Countless others have walked this path before you, grappling with the same emotions and uncertainties. Reach out to trusted friends, family members, or support groups who can offer empathy, understanding, and a shoulder to lean on.

Ultimately, navigating the rollercoaster of emotions that comes with loving someone with addiction requires self-compassion, patience, and grace. Allow yourself to feel what you're feeling without judgment or guilt. You're doing the best you can in an incredibly challenging situation, and that's something to be proud of.

How have your emotions been impacted by your experience of loving someone with addiction, and what strategies have you found helpful in navigating these complex feelings?

> ## To Summarize
>
> Examining the realities of addiction provides us with a candid portrayal of the complexities and challenges inherent in relationships affected by addiction. From the unpredictability and uncertainty to the emotional strain and self-centered behaviors, these realities shed light on the multifaceted nature of addiction's impact. By acknowledging these realities, we can begin to navigate our experiences with greater understanding and self-compassion. Moving forward, it's essential to prioritize self-care, set healthy boundaries, and seek support when needed, empowering ourselves to navigate the journey of loving someone struggling with addiction with resilience and courage.

·························· **Key Insights:** ··························

Unpredictable Nature of Addiction: Addiction is unpredictable and uncertain, leading to constant tension and anxiety within relationships. Addiction brings emotional turmoil, isolation, financial strain, and legal consequences, impacting both the addicted individual and their loved ones.

The Multifaceted Challenges of Addiction: A Closer Look at Its Ripple Effects. The self-centered nature of addiction can strain communication, erode trust, and create a sense of instability. Navigating addiction requires self-compassion, patience, and grace, allowing oneself to feel without judgment or guilt while seeking support from others who understand the journey.

Consolidating Our Insights: Understanding the patterns and emotional rollercoaster of addiction provides valuable insight for navigating tough relationship decisions. By knowing what you're up against, you gain clarity and awareness, empowering you to make informed choices. This knowledge serves as a foundation for enlightenment and self-discovery, offering a path toward self-awareness and empowerment. Ultimately, it supports you in navigating relationships affected by addiction by providing love and support, guiding you through the complexities with resilience and understanding.

Reflection: *As you reflect on your journey, how has gaining insight into the patterns and emotional rollercoaster of addiction helped you? Take a moment to consider how this understanding has empowered you to gain greater clarity and awareness. Looking ahead, how do you see yourself applying these insights to help navigate the complexities of relationships touched by addiction? What aspects of this journey resonate with you the most?*

CHAPTER 2

SAVING YOU IS KILLING ME

Accessing Your Relationship: Navigating Love Amidst Addiction's Challenges

Introduction

Welcome to the chapter where we dive headfirst into the turbulent waters of relationships entangled with addiction. This is not an easy journey, but you're not alone in navigating its choppy seas. Here, we'll unravel the intricate layers of how addiction disrupts the very fabric of relationships, leaving us grappling with a sense of disconnection and turmoil. Navigating a relationship affected by addiction is tough, to say the least.

Before we delve into this exploration, let's pause for a moment to reflect on a sentiment that may resonate deeply with many of us: "Saving You Is Killing Me." It's a phrase that encapsulates the profound paradox of loving someone struggling with addiction. At its core, it speaks to the agonizing dilemma of sacrificing our own well-being in the relentless pursuit of saving our loved ones from the grips of addiction. I frequently found myself uttering this statement, and you might find yourself doing the same.

Imagine being caught in the relentless tug-of-war between the desire to rescue your partner from the clutches of addiction and the gnawing realization that your efforts may be eroding your own sense of self-worth and happiness. It's a heart-wrenching conundrum that many of us have grappled with, and it's a testament to the depth of love and compassion we hold for those we care about.

In this chapter, we'll explore how addiction disrupts the alignment of our values and needs within relationships. We'll illuminate the subtle ways addiction-induced self-centeredness can warp our views, coaxing us into a cycle of codependency where our own needs and values take a backseat. But fear not, for amidst the chaos, there is clarity to be found.

Together, we'll unpack what it truly means to foster a healthy relationship grounded in mutual respect, trust, and authenticity. By understanding the essential components of a thriving bond, we'll gain a deeper appreciation for the complexities at play in relationships affected by addiction.

This chapter is focused on self-discovery, aiming to clarify our values and needs within the context of our relationships. By offering a fresh perspective, it enables us to navigate difficult relationship decisions more effectively. Through seeking perspective and cultivating a deeper understanding of our desires, we empower ourselves to confront future challenges with grace and resilience.

So, let's go on this transformative exploration together. As we navigate the complexities of love amidst addiction's challenges, may we find more clarity and emerge stronger, wiser, and more compassionate than ever before.

CHAPTER 2: SAVING YOU IS KILLING ME

Addiction's Impact on Relationships and the Misalignment of Values and Needs: A Recipe for Disaster

How has addiction impacted your own needs and values within your relationship? Have you found yourself prioritizing the addict's needs over your own, and if so, how has this affected your sense of self-worth and fulfillment?

In the tumultuous landscape of relationships affected by addiction, uncertainty often becomes a prevailing theme. It's akin to navigating through a dense fog where clarity is elusive, and the path ahead seems shrouded in mystery. Given the harsh realities of addiction—the emotional turmoil, unpredictability, and recurring patterns—it's natural to feel uncertain about the future of your relationship. This uncertainty stems from the profound impact addiction has on values and needs within relationships.

When we're in a relationship affected by addiction, the normal alignment of values and needs can be thrown into disarray. Addiction's selfish nature tends to prioritize the addict's cravings and desires above all else, including the needs and values of us loved ones. This creates a profound disconnect within the relationship, creating a recipe for disaster.

Imagine a scale where one side represents the addict's relentless pursuit of their addiction, and the other side represents our needs and values. In an ideal scenario, these elements would be balanced, with both parties' needs and values receiving equal consideration. However, addiction tilts the scale heavily in favor of the addiction, leaving the needs and values of loved ones neglected and overshadowed.

For example, let's say one of your core values in a relationship is respect. You value open communication, mutual understanding, and treating each other with kindness and consideration. However, addiction can erode these values by causing your addicted loved one to act in ways that are disrespectful or hurtful. They may lie, manipulate, or even engage in abusive behavior, prioritizing their addiction over your need for respect and kindness.

Similarly, addiction disrupts your basic needs, such as safety, security, and emotional well-being. You may find yourself sacrificing your own needs to accommodate the demands of the addiction, whether it's staying up late waiting for your addicted loved one to come home, tolerating verbal abuse because you empathize with their struggle, or neglecting your own self-care in favor of caretaking duties. You can see how addiction greatly impacts what we might be needing and what we might value in a relationship. Addiction profoundly influences our perceptions of what we need and value in a relationship. It distorts our priorities and skews our perception of what is important, often leading us to prioritize the addict's needs over our own. This can result in a significant misalignment between our true needs and values and the reality of our relationship dynamics.

In essence, addiction creates a dynamic where the addict's needs take precedence over all others, leading to a profound imbalance within the relationship. Your world becomes consumed by the relentless cycle of addiction, and you may find yourself losing sight of your own needs and values in the process. And saying things like " Saving You Is Killing Me."

Acknowledging the influence of addiction on your relationship is crucial, as is prioritizing your well-being amid the tumult it brings. Establishing boundaries, seeking support, and delving into your own needs and values are vital steps toward regaining control of your life amidst the chaos.

Navigating Needs and Values: Anchors in the Storm of Addiction

From a psychological perspective, needs are fundamental requirements for human well-being, encompassing both physical and emotional aspects. These needs are universal and essential for individuals to thrive.

Examples of needs include
Safety and Security: The need to feel safe and secure in one's environment, both physically and emotionally.

Connection and Belonging: The need for meaningful relationships and a sense of belonging within a community or social group.

Autonomy and Independence: The need to have a sense of control over one's life and decisions, as well as the freedom to express oneself authentically.

Esteem and Recognition: The need to feel valued, respected, and appreciated for one's contributions and qualities.

Purpose and Meaning: The need to find meaning and fulfillment in life, often through pursuing personal passions, goals, and aspirations.

Values, on the other hand, represent deeply held beliefs and principles that guide behavior and decision-making. They serve as a compass for how individuals prioritize their time, energy, and resources.

Examples of values include
Honesty and Integrity: Valuing truthfulness and moral uprightness in oneself and others.

Compassion and Empathy: Valuing kindness, understanding, and consideration for others' experiences and emotions.

Authenticity and Authentic Expression: Valuing genuineness and sincerity in one's thoughts, feelings, and actions.

Resilience and Perseverance: Valuing the ability to overcome challenges and adversity with determination and courage.

Connection and Relationships: Valuing meaningful connections with others and prioritizing nurturing and maintaining healthy relationships.

Understanding needs and values is especially important in the context of loving someone with addiction because addiction often disrupts these fundamental aspects of the human experience. For example:

Needs Disruption: Addiction can compromise an individual's ability to meet their own needs for safety, connection, and autonomy, as their focus becomes consumed by obtaining and using the addictive substance or engaging in addictive behaviors. Similarly, the needs of loved ones may be neglected or overshadowed by the demands of the addiction.

Values Conflict: Addiction-induced behaviors, such as deceit, manipulation, and neglect, can clash with values such as honesty, trust, and compassion. This can create internal conflict for both the individual struggling with addiction and their loved ones, leading to feelings of guilt, resentment, and moral distress.

By understanding needs and values, individuals can gain clarity on what is truly important to them and how addiction may be impacting their ability to honor these priorities. This awareness can serve as a foundation for setting boundaries, making decisions aligned with personal values, and prioritizing self-care in the face of addiction's challenges. Additionally, it can foster empathy and self-compassion in relationships affected by addiction, facilitating healthier communication and personal well-being.

In the context of your relationship affected by addiction, how have you noticed a misalignment between your needs and values and the reality of your relationship dynamics?

The Selfish Nature Of Addiction

You're in a battle against addiction—an adversary that prioritizes its own desires above all else. Addiction is inherently selfish; it demands allegiance and obedience, leaving little room for anything or anyone else. This selfish nature often manifests as addiction-induced narcissism, where the addict's focus becomes entirely consumed by their cravings and behaviors.

In the throes of addiction, addicts often become blind to the needs and values of those around them. Your needs, your desires, your well-being—they pale in comparison to the relentless demands of addiction. It's a heartbreaking realization to confront, feeling as though your struggles and concerns are dismissed or ignored in favor of the addiction's insatiable appetite.

Preserving your sanity becomes a huge task in itself. I've been there—I know the feeling of being stretched to the breaking point, desperately trying to defend your boundaries and fight for fair treatment. It's a constant battle against a force that seems insurmountable, leaving you drained and depleted both mentally and emotionally.

Actions speak louder than words

Actions speak louder than words, they say, and in the realm of addiction, this rings painfully true. Your loved one may profess their love and devotion to you, but their actions often tell a different story. They may promise change and improvement, only to fall back into old patterns and behaviors, leaving you bewildered and hurt. It's a cycle of hope and disappointment, with each flicker of love or progress quickly extinguished by the harsh reality of addiction's grip.

You're in a battle against addiction—an adversary that prioritizes its own desires above all else. Addiction is inherently selfish; it demands allegiance and obedience, leaving little room for anything or anyone else. This selfish nature often manifests as addiction-induced narcissism, where the addict's focus becomes entirely consumed by their cravings and behaviors. As the pressure cooker of emotions continues to build, frustration and depletion become your constant companions. You pour your energy and efforts into helping, saving, and fixing, only to find yourself further depleted because your own needs remain unmet. It's a downward spiral of despair and exhaustion, leaving you feeling trapped and powerless in the face of addiction's relentless onslaught.

The Healthy Relationship: Components of a Healthy Relationship

Navigating the complexities of relationships affected by addiction can feel like an uphill battle, and it's perfectly natural to feel overwhelmed by the daunting challenges ahead. But amidst the chaos, it's essential to remind ourselves of what a healthy relationship looks like—a beacon of hope and possibility in the midst of uncertainty.

Let's take a moment to reflect on the essential components of a healthy relationship—a relationship built on trust, respect, and mutual support. In a healthy relationship, communication flows freely, conflicts are resolved constructively, and both partners feel valued and appreciated for who they are. It's a partnership founded on love and understanding, where each individual's needs are considered and honored.

Several key elements contribute to a healthy relationship:

Trust: Trust forms the foundation of a healthy relationship. It involves reliability, honesty, and openness between partners. Trusting each other creates a sense of security and safety.

Communication: Effective communication is essential for understanding each other's thoughts, feelings, and needs. It involves active listening, expressing oneself clearly, and resolving conflicts constructively.

Respect: Mutual respect means valuing each other's opinions, boundaries, and autonomy. It involves treating each other with kindness, empathy, and consideration.

Equality: Healthy relationships are built on a foundation of equality, where both partners have an equal say in decision-making and share responsibilities fairly.

Support: Partners in a healthy relationship support each other's goals, dreams, and well-being. They provide emotional, practical, and moral support during both good times and challenges.

Independence: Healthy relationships allow each partner to maintain their individuality and independence. They respect each other's need for personal space, hobbies, and friendships outside the relationship.

Shared Values: While partners may have differences, they should share core values and goals that align with each other's aspirations and life direction.

Empathy: Empathy involves understanding and validating each other's emotions, perspectives, and experiences. It fosters connection, compassion, and emotional intimacy.

Compromise: Healthy relationships involve compromise and flexibility. Partners work together to find solutions that meet both of their needs and reach agreements that benefit the relationship as a whole.

Affection: Expressing love, affection, and appreciation is vital in a healthy relationship. Small gestures of kindness, physical touch, and verbal affirmations strengthen the bond between partners.

Overall, a healthy relationship is characterized by mutual respect, trust, communication, support, and shared values, allowing both partners to grow and thrive together.

Now, let's contrast these healthy relationship dynamics with those affected by addiction. There were many instances when I found myself imagining being a bystander, observing the relationship dynamics, and how my partner was treating me at that moment. If I could see it from an outsider's perspective, I might have been appalled. Perhaps you've had similar thoughts. But there's no shame in acknowledging this. Addiction is a complex issue, and like me, you may have clung to hope—the hope for the person they once were, the potential for recovery, and so forth.

Addiction distorts these fundamental elements, eroding trust, undermining communication, and causing profound disconnect between partners. In this context, the addict's cravings and behaviors often take precedence, leaving little room for the needs and values of their loved ones.

But fear not, for gaining clarity on what constitutes a healthy relationship can be a powerful tool in navigating the challenges ahead. By understanding what is important to you, what you value, and what you desire for yourself in a relationship, you can reclaim your sense of agency and empowerment.

This journey of self-discovery will empower you in countless ways. You'll gain self-awareness, allowing you to recognize and honor your own needs and values. You'll develop a deeper understanding of yourself and your desires, enabling you to make informed decisions that align with your well-being and happiness.

Most importantly, you'll reclaim your power—the power to take control of your own needs, the power to set boundaries that protect your well-being, and the power to cultivate relationships that uplift and support you. So as we embark on this journey together, let's hold onto the vision of a healthy relationship as a guiding light, illuminating the path toward healing, growth, and fulfillment.

Reflecting on the components of a healthy relationship, how do you feel your current relationship dynamics align with these principles? Are there areas where you feel there's room for improvement?

Clarifying Values: What Matters Most to You?

Now, let's seize this opportunity to clarify your values: What truly matters most to you? This process involves identifying your core values and relationship priorities. By seeking perspective and exploring the type of relationship you desire, you'll gain invaluable insights into your needs and desires.

Clarifying your values and needs is essential when navigating tough relationship decisions, whether you're deciding to stay, go, or find a middle ground. It empowers you to advocate for your own needs and remain true to what you value and know you deserve, regardless of the outcome.

To help you in this journey of self-discovery, consider engaging in a reflective exercise or activity. Take some time to jot down the values that resonate most deeply with you, reflecting on what truly matters in your relationships. Ask yourself probing questions, such as: What qualities do I value most in a partner? What are my non-negotiables in a relationship? What brings me a sense of fulfillment and joy in my interactions with others?

Through this process, you'll gain clarity on what matters most to you, empowering you to make decisions that align with your values and prioritize your well-being in all your relationships.

Values Assessment Tools

A values assessment tool is a resource designed to help individuals identify and prioritize their core values. These tools typically present a list of values or qualities and ask users to reflect on which ones resonate most strongly with them. Users may rank or select values based on their personal importance, allowing them to gain insight into what matters most to them in various areas of life, such as relationships, career, and personal development. Values assessment tools can be valuable for self-reflection, goal-setting, and decision-making, as they help individuals align their actions and choices with their deeply held beliefs and priorities.

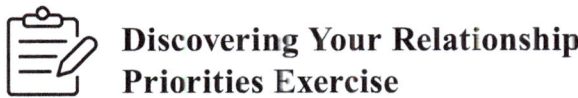
Discovering Your Relationship Priorities Exercise

Introduction:
Before making any significant decisions about your relationship, it's essential to clarify your values and priorities. This values assessment tool will help you identify what matters most to you in your relationships, guiding you toward greater clarity and empowerment.

Instructions:

Set aside some quiet time and find a comfortable space where you can focus without distractions.

Review the list of values provided below and consider each one carefully.

For each value, rate its importance to you on a scale from 1 to 10, with 1 being least important and 10 being most important. Be honest with yourself and trust your instincts.

After rating each value, reflect on your responses and identify any patterns or themes that emerge.

Use your ratings to prioritize your values, focusing on those that scored highest.

Consider how these prioritized values align with your current relationship dynamics and what changes, if any, you may want to make moving forward.

List of Values:	Scoring Example:
(You're welcome to explore available lists of values.)	
Honesty	Honesty: 9
Trust	Trust: 10
Communication	Communication: 8
Respect	Respect: 9
Empathy	Empathy: 10
Compassion	Compassion: 9
Support	Support: 8
Independence	Independence: 7
Intimacy	Intimacy: 9
Loyalty	Loyalty: 10
Equality	Equality: 8
Authenticity	Authenticity: 9
Forgiveness	Forgiveness: 7
Freedom	Freedom: 6
Security	Security: 9
Adventure	Adventure: 7
Growth	Growth: 8
Family	Family: 10
Health	Health: 9
Spirituality	Spirituality: 8

Reflection Questions:

What values emerged as the highest priorities for you?

How do these values influence your current relationship dynamics?

Are there any values that you feel are currently lacking or underrepresented in your relationship?

How can you integrate your prioritized values into your interactions and decisions within your relationship?

What steps can you take to honor your values and prioritize your well-being moving forward?

Take your time with this assessment, and remember that your values may evolve over time. Use this tool as a guide to gain insight into what matters most to you in your relationships and empower yourself to make decisions aligned with your values and priorities.

Clarifying Needs: What Do You Need Most For Yourself?

In the midst of navigating the complexities of a relationship affected by addiction, it's easy to lose sight of our own needs amidst the chaos. Yet, understanding what we truly need and want for ourselves is not only empowering but essential for our well-being, regardless of the decisions we face in our relationships.

This section invites you to go on a dive into self-discovery and introspection through a powerful exercise: the Self-Check-In. By taking a moment to pause and reflect on your needs, wants, and feelings, you can gain invaluable insights into what is essential for your personal growth and fulfillment.

Knowing what you need and want for yourself is akin to holding the key to your own empowerment. It allows you to advocate for your well-being, set boundaries, and make decisions that honor your values and priorities. As you engage in this exercise, you may be surprised by the clarity and strength that arises from simply acknowledging and honoring your inner experiences.

For example, imagine feeling exhausted after a sleepless night and a long day at work. By recognizing this feeling and identifying the need for rest, you empower yourself to take action and prioritize self-care by taking the afternoon off. This simple act of self-awareness and self-advocacy can have a profound impact on your overall well-being and resilience.

So, let's delve into the depths of our own needs, wants, and feelings and emerge with a newfound sense of empowerment and clarity.

 ## Self-Check-In Exercise: Identifying Your Needs, Wants, and Feelings

Introduction:
This exercise is designed to help you check in with yourself regularly, allowing you to identify your needs, wants, and feelings in the context of your relationship affected by addiction. By tuning into your inner experiences, you can gain greater clarity and insight into what you require to thrive and make informed decisions moving forward.

Instructions:
Find a quiet and comfortable space where you can sit undisturbed for a few minutes.

Take a few deep breaths to center yourself and bring your focus inward.

Begin by asking yourself the following questions:

- What am I needing right now in my relationship?
- What are my deepest desires and wants in this situation?
- How am I feeling emotionally at this moment?

Take your time to reflect on each question, allowing your thoughts and feelings to arise naturally.

Write down your responses in a journal or notebook, using bullet points or short sentences to capture your thoughts concisely.

Once you have completed the exercise, take a moment to review your answers and notice any common themes or patterns that emerge.

Consider how your current needs, wants, and feelings align with your values and priorities in your relationship.

Use this awareness to inform your interactions and decisions moving forward, prioritizing self-care and advocating for your own well-being.

Example Responses:

Needing: Support, understanding, reassurance, boundaries

Wanting: Open communication, honesty, respect, intimacy

Feeling: Anxious, overwhelmed, hopeful, frustrated

Reflection Questions:

How do my current needs align with my values and priorities in my relationship?

Are there any needs or wants that are not being met, and how can I address them?

What actions can I take to honor my feelings and advocate for my well-being?

How can I communicate my needs and desires effectively to my partner or support system?

What self-care practices can I incorporate into my daily routine to nurture my emotional health and resilience?

Remember to revisit this exercise regularly to stay connected with your inner experiences and continue prioritizing your well-being in your journey, both within and outside of your relationship. This check-in tool is a valuable resource that you can utilize at any time, irrespective of your relationship status. Taking the time to check in with yourself regularly is a powerful practice that fosters self-awareness, empowerment, and personal growth. So, make it a habit to pause, reflect, and honor your needs, wants, and feelings on a consistent basis.

To Summarize:

In this chapter, we talked about the complexities of love amidst addiction's challenges. We delved deep into the turbulent waters of relationships entangled with addiction, unraveling the layers of how addiction disrupts the very fabric of our connections. It's a journey fraught with uncertainty, heartache, and self-discovery, but one that ultimately leads to greater clarity, empowerment, and compassion.

We began by acknowledging the profound paradox of loving someone struggling with addiction—the agonizing dilemma of sacrificing our own well-being in the relentless pursuit of saving our loved ones. The phrase "Saving You Is Killing Me" encapsulates this struggle, resonating deeply with many who have grappled with the complexities of addiction in their relationships.

Through our exploration, we illuminated how addiction disrupts the alignment of our values and needs within relationships, creating a profound disconnect and imbalance. Addiction's selfish nature prioritizes the addict's cravings and behaviors above all else, leaving little room for the needs and values of their loved ones. Yet, amidst the chaos, there is clarity to be found.

We unpacked what it truly means to foster a healthy relationship grounded in trust, respect, and mutual support. By understanding the essential components of a thriving bond, we gained a deeper appreciation for the complexities at play in relationships affected by addiction.

Throughout this journey, we clarified our values and needs within the context of our relationships, empowering ourselves to make informed decisions aligned with our well-being and happiness. By seeking perspective and cultivating a deeper understanding of our desires, we can confront future challenges with grace and resilience.

As we conclude this chapter, let us hold onto the vision of a healthy relationship as a guiding light, illuminating the path toward healing, growth, and fulfillment. May we continue to navigate the complexities of love amidst addiction's challenges with self-compassion, courage and self-awareness, emerging stronger, wiser, and more empowered than ever before.

Key Insights

Acknowledging the Paradox: Loving someone struggling with addiction often involves sacrificing our own well-being in the pursuit of saving them—a profound paradox that requires deep self-reflection and compassion.

Disruption of Values and Needs: Addiction disrupts the alignment of our values and needs within relationships, prioritizing the addict's cravings and behaviors above all else and creating a profound disconnect and imbalance.

Fostering Healthy Relationships: Understanding the essential components of a healthy relationship—grounded in trust, respect, and mutual support—empowers us to navigate the challenges of addiction with grace and resilience.

Empowerment through Self-Discovery: Clarifying our values and needs within the context of our relationships empowers us to make informed decisions aligned with our well-being and happiness, fostering self-awareness, and resilience.

Consolidating Our Insights: Understanding addiction's impact on relationships, recognizing the components of a healthy relationship, and knowing your values and needs are essential for navigating tough relationship decisions. This information provides a framework for assessing the health of your relationship and evaluating whether it aligns with your values and needs. By gaining clarity on these aspects, you empower yourself with self-awareness and clarity, enabling you to make informed decisions about staying or leaving. It fosters enlightenment and self-discovery by guiding you to understand your desires and priorities, ultimately supporting you in navigating tough relationship decisions touched by addiction with love and support.

> **Reflection:** *How has learning about addiction's effects on relationships, recognizing what makes a healthy relationship, and understanding your own values and needs helped you? Take a moment to think about how this knowledge has given you clarity and power to assess your relationships. Looking ahead, how do you see yourself using this understanding to handle future challenges in relationships impacted by addiction?*

CHAPTER 3

IT'LL GET BETTER. OR WILL IT?

Navigating Love's Toughest Moments: Hope and Reality

Introduction

Welcome to this chapter, where we're diving deep into the heart of relationships tangled up in addiction. It's a tough journey, where hope and reality sometimes feel like they're at odds.

Have you ever felt like you're pushing a rope or talking to a wall when dealing with addiction? It's frustrating, right? In this chapter, we're going to talk about those moments—when hope meets harsh truths, and we're left wondering how to navigate it all.

We'll start by looking at why we stick around in relationships affected by addiction. It's not always easy, but love, commitment, and a desire to help our loved ones are often the driving forces. But sometimes, that care and kindness can leave us feeling stuck, like we're not making any progress.

And let's talk about hope. It's a powerful thing, but it can also blind us to the reality of addiction. We'll explore how to strike a balance between hope and realism, so we can face the truth head-on.

Confronting the harsh reality of addiction isn't something any of us want to do, but it's necessary. It means letting go of the illusions we've held onto and facing the truth, even when it's hard. But in doing so, we empower ourselves to take control of our own well-being.

Finally, we'll tackle the internal struggle of feeling responsible for our loved ones' well-being. It's a tough balancing act, but by caring for ourselves and setting boundaries, we can create healthier relationships and a brighter future for ourselves and our loved ones.

Swimming Upstream Against Addiction's Tide

I kept saying to myself; it's like talking to a wall or pushing a rope being with an addict. Let's explore what I mean by all these expressions: In the context of loving someone who struggles with addiction, the expression "pushing a rope" vividly captures the feeling of helplessness and frustration that often accompanies our efforts to support them. Just as it's impossible to push a limp rope forward, no matter how hard you try, attempting to compel or guide someone struggling with addiction to change can feel equally futile.

When we're in a relationship with an addict, we may find ourselves constantly trying to persuade, convince, or control their behavior, hoping to steer them away from destructive habits. However, addiction is a powerful force that resists such efforts, often rendering our attempts ineffective. All of this can leave us feeling hopeless.

CHAPTER 3: IT'LL GET BETTER. OR WILL IT?

Despite our best intentions and heartfelt efforts, we may feel as though we're met with resistance, denial, or relapse at every turn. It's a draining and demoralizing experience, leaving us feeling exhausted, discouraged, and questioning whether our efforts are making any difference at all.

The metaphor of "pushing a rope" serves as a reminder of the limitations of our influence over someone else's addiction. It prompts us to recognize the importance of focusing on what we can control—our own actions, boundaries, and well-being—rather than expending energy on fruitless attempts to change someone else.

Ultimately, acknowledging the reality of "pushing a rope" can be a catalyst for shifting our perspective and redirecting our efforts toward self-care, acceptance, and seeking support. It's about recognizing our own limitations while also acknowledging the complexity of addiction and the need for self-compassionate, self-care and courage while navigating our relationships.

In your experience, have you ever felt like you were 'pushing a rope' in a relationship affected by addiction? If so, what emotions and challenges did you encounter while trying to influence or support your loved one's behavior?

Why We Stay: The Strength of Commitment Amidst Adversity

In the realm of relationships entangled with addiction, the concept of staying despite immense challenges becomes a testament to the depth of our commitment. Like the age-old vows of "till death do us part" and promises to stand by each other through thick and thin, we find ourselves holding onto love and loyalty in the face of adversity.

You may have caught yourself reassuring, "It'll get better," clinging to hope for the return of our loved one and a return to normalcy in our lives. I, too, often told myself this to ease my worries and maintain optimism for a brighter future. However, the sad reality is that things didn't improve; they only worsened. Perhaps you find yourself in a similar situation.

It's natural to offer ourselves these comforting assurances, but it's crucial to acknowledge the possibility that things might not improve. Balancing hope with realism is essential for navigating a relationship affected by addiction.

The mantra of "It'll get better" kept me in the relationship far longer than I should have stayed. Recognizing this, I've learned the importance of tempering optimism with a realistic viewpoint to make informed decisions about my well-being and the dynamics of the relationship.

Exploring the deep-rooted reasons for remaining steadfast in a relationship affected by addiction unveils the profound strength of commitment amidst turmoil. At the core of our decision to stay lies a genuine desire to support and protect our loved ones, fueled by the bonds of love and the promise of better days ahead.

Here's a list of various reasons why we might choose to stay in a relationship affected by addiction

Love: Despite the challenges, individuals may deeply love their partner and believe in their potential for recovery.

Commitment: They are committed to their partner and the relationship, vowing to stand by them through thick and thin.

Hope: Holding onto hope for a better future, believing that their partner can overcome addiction with support and treatment.

Sense of Duty: Feeling a sense of duty or responsibility to support their partner through their struggles.

Fear of Abandonment: They fear that leaving their partner will worsen their addiction or lead to negative consequences.

Financial Dependence: Financial entanglement with their partner may make it difficult to leave, such as shared assets or financial support.

Cultural or Religious Beliefs: Cultural or religious beliefs may prioritize the sanctity of marriage and discourage divorce or separation.

Children: Concern for the well-being of children or the desire to maintain a stable family environment may keep individuals in the relationship.

Emotional Attachment: Despite the challenges, individuals may feel emotionally attached to their partner and struggle to let go.

Optimism: They may remain optimistic about their partner's ability to change and overcome addiction in the future.

Fear of Loneliness: The fear of being alone or starting over in a new relationship may deter individuals from leaving.

Guilt: Feeling guilty about leaving their partner during a difficult time or feeling responsible for their well-being.

Enabling Behavior: Unintentionally enabling their partner's addiction by providing financial, emotional, or logistical support.

Lack of Support Network: Limited support from friends or family may make it difficult for individuals to leave the relationship.

Co-dependency: Developing a co-dependent relationship dynamic where individuals feel responsible for their partner's happiness and well-being.

Perceived Social Pressure: Concerns about how leaving the relationship will be perceived by others or fear of judgment from society.

History and Memories: Fond memories of the relationship's happier times or nostalgia for the past may influence individuals to stay.

Emotional Investment: The emotional investment in the relationship and the hope that things will improve over time.

Dependency: Individuals may depend on their partner for emotional support, companionship, or a sense of identity.

Denial: Denying the severity of the addiction or the impact it has on the relationship, hoping that things will improve without intervention.

Have you ever found yourself holding onto hope and loyalty in the face of adversity, much like the age-old vows of 'till death do us part'? What deep-rooted reasons resonate with you when it comes to staying in a relationship touched by addiction?

The Pitfalls of Optimism: Understanding the Limitations of Positive Thinking

In your journey of supporting a loved one struggling with addiction, have you ever experienced the pitfalls of optimism? What were they?

Navigating a relationship affected by addiction often involves walking a delicate tightrope between hope and realism. While optimism can be a source of strength and resilience, it's essential to recognize its limitations and the potential pitfalls of overly positive thinking.

Maintaining hope in the face of addiction is no easy feat. It requires us to believe in the possibility of recovery and positive change despite the overwhelming challenges and setbacks we may encounter along the way. However, blind optimism can sometimes lead us down a dangerous path, blinding us to the harsh realities of addiction and its impact on our lives.

The pitfalls of optimism become apparent when we fail to balance hope with realism. In our fervent desire for a better future, we may overlook warning signs, minimize the severity of the situation, or ignore our own needs and boundaries. This can result in poor decision-making and enablement of destructive behaviors, ultimately prolonging the cycle of addiction and suffering.

Balancing hope with realism requires us to acknowledge the harsh truths of addiction while still holding onto the belief in the possibility of recovery. It involves facing the difficult realities head-on, such as the relapses, the lies, and the emotional turmoil, without losing sight of our own well-being and boundaries.

By embracing a balanced perspective, we can navigate the complexities of loving someone with addiction with greater clarity and resilience. We can hold onto hope while also setting realistic expectations and boundaries, empowering ourselves to make informed decisions that prioritize our own well-being and the well-being of our loved ones.

Optimism can backfire in the context of addiction in several ways

Ignoring Warning Signs: Optimism may lead individuals to overlook or minimize warning signs of addiction, such as secretive behavior, mood swings, or financial problems.

Enabling Destructive Behavior: Optimism can enable individuals to downplay the severity of their loved one's addiction and inadvertently support their destructive behaviors, such as providing financial assistance or making excuses for their actions.

False Expectations: Excessive optimism can create unrealistic expectations for recovery, leading individuals to believe that their loved one will overcome addiction quickly and easily, without recognizing the long and challenging journey ahead.

Emotional Drain: Maintaining unwavering optimism can be emotionally draining, especially when faced with repeated disappointments and setbacks in the recovery process.

Neglecting Self-Care: Optimism may cause individuals to prioritize their loved one's needs over their own, neglecting their own well-being and boundaries in the process.

Denial of Reality: Excessive optimism can lead to denial of the harsh realities of addiction, preventing individuals from seeking help or taking necessary actions to protect themselves and their loved ones.

False Sense of Control: Optimism may give individuals a false sense of control over the situation, leading them to believe that their positive thinking alone can solve the problem of addiction.

Delaying Necessary Interventions: Overly optimistic individuals may delay seeking professional help or intervention for their loved one, believing that things will improve on their own without outside assistance.

Disappointment and Resentment: When optimistic expectations are not met, individuals may experience feelings of disappointment, resentment, and betrayal, further straining their relationship with their loved one.

Reinforcing Codependency: Optimism can reinforce codependent relationship dynamics, where individuals feel responsible for their loved one's happiness and well-being, even at the expense of their own.

Confronting the Reality: When Hope Backfires and Self-Preservation is Necessary

Hope is a powerful and positive emotion that can uplift us in times of adversity, infusing us with optimism and resilience. It's a beacon of light in the darkest of moments, guiding us through uncertainty and hardship. In the context of relationships affected by addiction, hope often serves as a lifeline, sustaining our belief in the possibility of recovery and redemption.

The Power of Hope: Hope inspires us to persevere through tough times, reminding us that better days may lie ahead. It fuels our determination and fuels our commitment to our loved ones, encouraging us to stand by them in their darkest moments. It gives us strength when we feel overwhelmed and reminds us of the love and connection that bind us together.

The Pitfalls of Excessive Hope: However, there comes a point where hope can turn into a double-edged sword, leading us down a path of denial and disillusionment. When hope blinds us to the harsh realities of addiction, it can keep us trapped in unhealthy relationships and prevent us from taking necessary action to protect ourselves. Confronting the reality of addiction means acknowledging the limitations of hope and recognizing when it's time to prioritize our own well-being. It means bravely facing the truth, even when it's painful, and making difficult decisions for our own sake.

Balancing Hope and Reality: Finding the balance between hope and reality is a delicate dance—one that requires courage, honesty, and self-awareness. It's about holding onto hope for a better future while also accepting the limitations of the present moment. It's about honoring our emotions and intuition while also trusting our judgment and setting healthy boundaries.

Empowering Self-Preservation

Above all, confronting the reality of addiction empowers us to prioritize our own well-being and self-preservation. It's about shifting our focus from hoping for others' behavior to change to cultivating hope for a better future for ourselves. This distinction is crucial—it's about recognizing that we cannot control the actions of others, but we can control how we choose to navigate our own lives.

Choosing self-preservation and prioritizing self-wellness in how we approach hope empowers us. It's about recognizing that we deserve to be happy and healthy, regardless of the circumstances of our relationships. It's about reclaiming our agency and autonomy, even in the face of addiction's grip.

Agency refers to our ability to make independent choices and take actions that influence our lives. It's about recognizing that we have control over our own thoughts, emotions, and behaviors, even when faced with challenging circumstances. Reclaiming our agency means asserting ourselves as active participants in our own lives rather than passive bystanders.

Autonomy is closely related to agency but emphasizes our right to self-governance and freedom from external control. It's about honoring our own values, preferences, and boundaries, even in the presence of external pressures or influences. Reclaiming our autonomy means asserting our right to make decisions that align with our own best interests and well-being.

Instead of pinning our hopes on someone else's recovery, we invest in our own growth, healing, and fulfillment. We recognize that we have the power to shape our own destiny and prioritize our own well-being, independent of the choices made by our loved ones struggling with addiction. By reclaiming our agency and autonomy, we take ownership of our lives and encourage a journey of self-discovery, empowerment, and personal growth.

By prioritizing our own well-being, we reclaim our agency and autonomy. We acknowledge that we have the power to shape our own destiny, independent of the choices made by our loved ones struggling with addiction. It's a radical act of self-love and self-respect—an acknowledgment of our inherent worth and value.

Confronting the reality of addiction requires immense courage and inner strength. It's about facing our fears and uncertainties head-on, refusing to be defined by the challenges we face. Instead of being consumed by despair, we harness the power of hope to envision a brighter future for ourselves—a future filled with joy, purpose, and fulfillment.

In the journey of navigating relationships affected by addiction, empowering self-preservation is paramount. It's about shifting our focus from external factors to internal growth, from hoping for change in others to cultivating change within ourselves. By embracing this mindset, we unlock the potential for profound personal transformation and reclaim our rightful place as architects of our own happiness and well-being.

Have you ever found yourself clinging to hope, hoping for someone else's behavior to change, only to realize that true empowerment lies in focusing on your own well-being and future happiness?

Reclaiming Agency, Autonomy, and Checking in on Hope Exercise:

Reflective Journaling:
Take some time to reflect on your own experiences with hope, agency, and autonomy in the context of relationships affected by addiction. Answer the following questions in your journal:

- How has hope influenced your decision-making in relationships affected by addiction?

- Have you ever felt powerless or stuck, hoping for someone else's behavior to change?

- In what ways have you reclaimed agency and autonomy in your life?

- How can you shift your focus from external factors to internal growth and well-being?

Hope Inventory Exercise:
Create a hope inventory to assess the balance between hopeful thinking and realistic expectations. List your hopes and aspirations related to relationships affected by addiction, and then evaluate each one:

- Is this hope based on realistic expectations?

- How does this hope impact my sense of agency and autonomy?

- Are there any hopes that I need to let go of in order to prioritize my own well-being?

Hope Check-In:
Schedule regular check-ins to evaluate your relationship with hope and ensure that it aligns with your goals for agency and autonomy. Reflect on the following questions during your check-ins:

- How has my relationship with hope evolved since the last check-in?

- Have I noticed any patterns of excessive hope or unrealistic expectations?

- What adjustments can I make to maintain a healthy balance between hope and realism?

Remember to approach these exercises with compassion and self-reflection. Reclaiming agency and autonomy is a journey, and each step you take toward prioritizing your own well-being is a testament to your strength and resilience.

Navigating the Internal Conflict: Balancing Empathy and Self-Preservation

One of the most profound challenges we encounter when loving someone struggling with addiction is the internal conflict of feeling responsible for their well-being. We are driven by a deep sense of empathy and compassion, wanting to support and uplift our loved ones in their time of need. However, this noble intention can often lead us down a path of sacrificing our own well-being in the process. We want to be empathetic to their struggle, yet we also risk sacrificing our own well-being in the process. This conflict is exacerbated by conflicting messages about addiction being a disease, which sometimes leads us to feel conflicted about how much empathy to show and how much to tolerate destructive behaviors.

The Disease Model Dilemma: Guilt and Confusion

The prevalent understanding of addiction as a disease further complicates this internal struggle. While the disease model encourages compassion and empathy towards individuals battling addiction, it also fosters feelings of guilt and confusion. We may grapple with questions like, "If addiction is a disease, should I feel guilty for setting boundaries or prioritizing my own needs?" This conflict tests the limits of our empathy and challenges us to find a delicate balance between understanding and self-preservation.

Empathy Tested: The Internal Conflict Unveiled

At the heart of this internal conflict lies in the fear of letting our loved ones down. We feel a profound sense of responsibility for their well-being, often at the expense of our own. We wrestle with the desire to support them unconditionally while also acknowledging the importance of setting boundaries and prioritizing our own mental and emotional health.

The Urge to Save: Wrestling with the Illusion of Control

As compassionate and empathetic individuals, it's natural for us to want to save, fix, or rescue our addicted loved ones. We are driven by a genuine desire to alleviate their suffering and restore harmony to our relationships. However, this well-intentioned impulse can often lead us down a path of frustration and disillusionment.

The Illusion of Control: Recognizing Our Limits

Despite our best efforts, it's essential to recognize that we cannot control or cure addiction. Addiction is a complex and multifaceted disease with roots that extend far beyond our influence. We may find ourselves shouldering the burden of responsibility, believing that if we just try harder or love more, we can somehow "fix" the problem. However, this mindset only perpetuates the illusion of control and sets us up for disappointment when our efforts fall short.

Not Our Monkey, Not Our Circus: Embracing Reality

In reality, addiction is not our burden to bear. We did not cause it, and we cannot single-handedly solve it. It's crucial to acknowledge that while we can offer love, support, and encouragement, the journey to recovery ultimately lies in the hands of the individual struggling with addiction. As the saying goes, "Not our monkey, not our circus."

Finding Peace in Acceptance: Letting Go of Guilt and Resentment

By releasing ourselves from the unrealistic burden of responsibility, we free ourselves to focus on what we can control: our own well-being and the boundaries we set in our relationships. We can let go of feelings of guilt or resentment for not being able to "save" our loved ones and instead channel our energy into fostering a supportive and nurturing environment.

Empowering Ourselves: Prioritizing Self-Care and Boundaries

Empowerment begins with acceptance—acceptance of our limitations, acceptance of the reality of addiction, and acceptance of the inherent worth and dignity of ourselves and our loved ones. By prioritizing self-care, setting healthy boundaries, and relinquishing the need to control, we reclaim our agency and autonomy in the face of adversity.

Balancing Self-Preservation and Understanding

Finding equilibrium between empathy and self-preservation is essential for maintaining our own well-being while supporting our loved ones through their addiction journey. It requires us to recognize that while we can offer love, compassion, and support, we cannot control or "fix" their addiction for them. By setting healthy boundaries and prioritizing our own needs, we empower ourselves to be effective sources of support without sacrificing our own well-being.

In the intricate dance of loving someone struggling with addiction, balancing empathy and self-preservation is a constant journey of self-discovery and growth. By acknowledging the internal conflict we face and embracing the complexity of the disease model, we can navigate this challenging terrain with compassion and understanding. Ultimately, by prioritizing our own well-being while offering unwavering support to our loved ones, we create a foundation for healing and resilience for both parties involved.

To Summarize

Navigating relationships entangled in addiction is a challenging journey where hope and reality often clash. It's a journey marked by internal conflicts, emotional turmoil, and the constant struggle to find balance. However, amidst the chaos, there are valuable lessons to be learned and opportunities for personal growth and empowerment. Navigating relationships affected by addiction requires courage, compassion, and self-awareness. By embracing the complexities of addiction, prioritizing self-care, and finding balance between empathy and self-preservation, you empower yourself to navigate this challenging terrain with grace and resilience. Remember, you are not alone on this journey, and by prioritizing your own well-being, you create the foundation for healing and transformation.

Key Insights:

Recognize the Limitations of Control: Acknowledge that addiction is not something we can control or cure. While we can offer support and encouragement, the journey to recovery ultimately lies with the individual struggling with addiction.

Tempering Optimism with Realism: Recognize the tendency to cling to the hope that things will improve, but also acknowledge the possibility that they may not. Balancing optimism with a realistic viewpoint is crucial for making informed decisions about your well-being and navigating relationships affected by addiction.

Balance Empathy with Realism: Find a delicate balance between empathy and realism. While it's essential to offer love and support to your loved one, it's equally important to confront the harsh realities of addiction and prioritize your own well-being.

Embrace Acceptance and Empowerment: Accept the reality of addiction and release yourself from the burden of responsibility. Empower yourself to focus on what you can control—your own actions, boundaries, and well-being. By reclaiming agency and autonomy, you create space for healing and growth for yourself and your loved ones.

Consolidating Our Insights: Reflecting on the "It'll get better" mindset and the potential drawbacks of excessive optimism can provide valuable insights for us as we navigate tough relationship decisions affected by addiction. By confronting the realities of addiction and embracing a balanced perspective that combines hope with realism, we can gain clarity and make more informed choices about staying or leaving a relationship. Confronting reality and maintaining hope are crucial for us to gain clarity, as they allow us to acknowledge the challenges while still believing in the possibility of positive change. Navigating internal conflicts between empathy and self-preservation also plays a significant role in deciding to stay or go, as we must balance our compassion for our loved one with our own well-being. Overall, these considerations contribute to our enlightenment and self-discovery by guiding us to understand our own needs and priorities. This self-awareness and clarity empower us to make tough relationship decisions with confidence and ultimately support us in navigating relationships affected by addiction with love and support.

Reflection: *How has your perspective on the "It'll get better" mindset evolved as you've learned more about addiction's impact on relationships? Reflect on how balancing hope with realism will help you in navigating tough relationship decisions. Additionally, consider the internal conflicts you've faced between empathy for your loved one and prioritizing your own well-being. How have these insights contributed to your self-awareness and clarity?*

CHAPTER 4

BRUISED HEART

Unmasking Shadows: Recognizing Abuse and Unhealthy Patterns

Introduction

In this chapter, we will delve into the often overlooked but critically important topic of recognizing abuse and unhealthy patterns in relationships affected by addiction. While addiction itself poses significant challenges, it can also create fertile ground for various forms of abuse and dysfunctional dynamics to flourish. By shining a light on these shadows, we empower ourselves to identify, address, and ultimately break free from toxic patterns that perpetuate suffering and hinder our ability to heal.

The dynamic of addiction within relationships often serves as a breeding ground for excusing, denying, or even accepting bad behavior. When faced with the consequences of their actions, individuals struggling with addiction may lean on the excuse of being intoxicated or not realizing what they were doing at the time. This pattern allows them to get away with harmful behavior, creating a recipe for disaster within the relationship. The disease model of addiction, while valuable in understanding addiction as a complex medical condition, can inadvertently perpetuate this mentality by providing a framework for justifying or minimizing the consequences of addictive behavior. However, it's crucial to recognize that abuse is abuse, regardless of the presence of addiction. Whether the behavior stems from addiction or not, it still inflicts harm and has a profound impact on the well-being of those involved. When deciding whether to stay, leave, or find a middle ground in a relationship affected by addiction, it's essential to be armed with this knowledge and to prioritize one's safety, dignity, and emotional well-being.

Understanding the Intersection of Addiction and Abuse

In reflecting on the intertwining of addiction and abuse in relationships, have you ever found yourself caught in a cycle of promises and disappointments, much like a rollercoaster ride? How did this tumultuous experience impact your emotional well-being and your perception of the relationship?

In the intricate web of relationships affected by addiction, there lies the potential for toxic dynamics to take root and thrive. These patterns, often concealed by the complexities of addiction, silently corrode the very essence of healthy relationships. It is crucial to unveil these hidden dynamics, to bring them into the light of awareness, and to acknowledge them as the essential first step in reclaiming personal strength and overall well-being. By bravely confronting these shadows that linger within our relationships, we not only liberate ourselves from their harmful grip but also empower ourselves to foster connections rooted in mutual respect, compassion, and vitality.

Abuse in a relationship can take various forms, spanning beyond substance abuse to include emotional, verbal, psychological, physical, sexual, and financial abuse. In relationships affected by addiction, these abusive behaviors can become intertwined or exacerbated by the challenges presented by the addictive behaviors. For instance, emotional and verbal abuse might intensify due to the emotional volatility often associated with addiction, while psychological abuse may stem from manipulation and control tactics related to addictive behaviors. Additionally, financial abuse may occur when the individual struggling with addiction prioritizes their addictive habits over financial responsibilities, leading to financial instability and exploitation within the relationship. Ultimately, addiction can amplify existing abusive patterns or introduce new forms of abuse, creating complex and challenging dynamics that impact the well-being of everyone involved.

Abuse encompasses a range of behaviors aimed at exerting power and control over another individual, often resulting in harm or distress.

Abuse can manifest in various forms, including

Physical abuse: Inflicting physical harm or injury on another person through actions such as hitting, punching, kicking, or restraining.

Emotional abuse: Using verbal attacks, threats, manipulation, or intimidation to undermine an individual's self-esteem, sense of worth, or emotional well-being.

Verbal abuse: Engaging in name-calling, insults, humiliation, or yelling to degrade or belittle the other person.

Psychological abuse: Employing tactics such as gaslighting, mind games, or emotional manipulation to confuse, control, or undermine the victim's mental stability.

Sexual abuse: Forcing or coercing someone into unwanted sexual activity or engaging in sexual acts without consent.

Financial abuse: Controlling or exploiting someone financially by withholding access to money, stealing assets, or coercing financial decisions.

Digital abuse: Using technology, such as social media, texting, or monitoring devices, to harass, stalk, or control the victim.

Abuse can occur in any relationship, regardless of age, gender, sexual orientation, or socioeconomic status. It is characterized by a pattern of behavior that seeks to dominate, intimidate, or harm the other person, often resulting in long-term physical, emotional, and psychological consequences. Recognizing the signs of abuse is essential for promoting safety, seeking support, and taking steps to address and prevent further harm.

Breaking the Cycle: Understanding the Interplay of Addiction and Abuse

The cyclical nature of addiction and abuse creates a tumultuous experience for individuals caught in its grip, akin to being on a rollercoaster or merry-go-round. In this cycle, addictive behaviors often lead to abusive actions, which, in turn, fuel further substance use or addictive behaviors. The constant ups and downs, twists and turns of this cycle can leave individuals feeling trapped and helpless, unable to break free from the destructive pattern.

I vividly remember the promises my addicted loved one made, reassuring me that things would be different this time. Yet, as the weekend approached, he would disappear without a trace, leaving me alone with my thoughts and fears. When he returned, it was as if nothing had happened. He showered me with affection, offering the love and attention I craved, and promising to make things right. But before long, a petty disagreement would escalate into a heated argument, and he would storm out, leaving me to spend another sleepless night alone. This cycle of promises and disappointments felt like a rollercoaster, constantly leaving me emotionally exhausted and uncertain about the future of our relationship.

It's crucial to recognize that abuse is abuse, regardless of the presence of addiction. Even if there is a tendency to excuse or justify abusive behavior due to addiction, it still has a profound impact on our well-being. Whether the abuse is fueled by substance abuse or other addictive behaviors, it erodes our sense of safety, self-worth, and dignity. No amount of addiction can excuse or justify the harm caused by abusive actions.

The disease model of addiction, while valuable in understanding addiction as a complex medical condition, can sometimes foster an excuse-out mentality. This mentality may lead individuals to minimize or rationalize abusive behavior as a symptom of their addiction, rather than taking responsibility for their actions. While addiction may contribute to certain behaviors, it does not absolve individuals of accountability for their choices. It's essential to separate the disease of addiction from the responsibility to address and rectify abusive behavior, recognizing that both issues require attention for healing and recovery to occur.

Unmasking Abusive and Unhealthy Dynamics

Within the intricacies of relationships affected by addiction, there exists the potential for unhealthy dynamics to take root and flourish. These patterns, often obscured by the challenges of addiction, can silently erode the very foundation upon which relationships are built. It is imperative to unveil these insidious dynamics, to expose them to the light of awareness, and to recognize them as the crucial initial step in reclaiming our personal strength and overall well-being. By courageously confronting these shadows that linger within our relationships, we not only break free from their toxic grip but also empower ourselves to foster connections that are rooted in respect, compassion, and health.

The Subtle Veil of Unhealthy Patterns

Addiction's complexities can create an environment where unhealthy patterns thrive. These patterns may manifest in various ways, such as emotional manipulation, control, verbal abuse, or neglect. The stressors and uncertainties brought about by addiction can mask these behaviors, making them appear as justifiable responses to challenging circumstances. Yet, beneath this veil lies the truth—a truth that must be faced head-on to preserve the integrity of the relationship and the well-being of all involved.

Addiction's complexities can indeed foster an environment where unhealthy patterns can flourish within relationships.

Here are some examples illustrating how addiction's complexities can contribute to the emergence of unhealthy patterns:

Emotional Rollercoaster: The unpredictability of an addicted loved one's moods due to substance use or withdrawal can lead to an emotional rollercoaster for both individuals. This constant upheaval might result in the non-addicted person walking on eggshells or altering their behavior to avoid triggering negative reactions.

Isolation and Secrecy: The shame and stigma often associated with addiction can lead to secrecy and isolation. The addicted individual might hide their substance use, leading to distrust and suspicion. In response, the non-addicted person might become overly vigilant, trying to uncover the truth, which can create an atmosphere of secrecy and mistrust.

Blurred Boundaries: Addiction can blur the boundaries between individuals, making it difficult to differentiate between personal needs and the needs of the relationship. This can result in codependent behaviors, where one person's emotional well-being becomes contingent on the other's actions, leading to an unhealthy dynamic.

Escalation of Conflict: The strain that addiction puts on relationships can lead to escalated conflicts. Disagreements might turn into heated arguments, with hurtful words exchanged as a way to cope with frustration and pain. These intense conflicts can damage the emotional safety within the relationship.

Manipulative Behavior: Addiction-driven cravings can lead to manipulative behavior, where the addicted individual attempts to gain sympathy or manipulate situations to satisfy their cravings. This can result in the non-addicted person feeling used and manipulated, leading to a breakdown of trust.

Financial Strain: Addiction often comes with financial repercussions, as funds are diverted towards acquiring substances. Financial strain can lead to disagreements over money, power imbalances, and resentment between individuals.

Neglect of Responsibilities: The all-consuming nature of addiction can lead to neglect of responsibilities such as work, household chores, and childcare. This neglect can cause frustration and resentment to build up, contributing to an environment of dysfunction.

Disrupted Communication: Addiction-related stress and emotions can disrupt effective communication. Misunderstandings might arise due to unclear or aggressive communication, leading to further strain on the relationship.

Loss of Intimacy: Intimacy, both emotional and physical, can be eroded by addiction. The focus on substances can lead to emotional distance, and the addicted individual might prioritize their addiction over maintaining intimacy.

Cycle of Promises and Disappointments: The addicted individual might promise to change or quit using substances, only to relapse shortly afterward. This cycle of promises and disappointments can erode trust and cause emotional turmoil for both individuals.

Control and Manipulation: Unhealthy dynamics can manifest as attempts to control the addicted individual's actions and decisions under the guise of concern. For instance, using guilt or threats to manipulate their choices or prevent them from seeking help.

Verbal or Emotional Abuse: Addiction-related stress may lead to emotional outbursts or insults, constituting verbal abuse. It's essential to recognize when such behavior becomes a pattern and not just a reaction to stress.

Neglect of Well-Being: In the shadow of addiction, the needs and well-being of individuals can be overlooked. This neglect can perpetuate an unhealthy dynamic where one person's struggles dominate the relationship's focus.

Recognizing these examples underscores the need to address these unhealthy patterns. By acknowledging the role of addiction in fostering these dynamics, individuals can take proactive steps towards healing, setting boundaries, seeking support, and cultivating healthier interactions.

Actions Speak Louder Than Words

Have you ever found yourself in a situation where the actions of your loved one struggling with addiction contradicted their words or promises? How did this discrepancy between words and actions impact your perception of the relationship and your emotional well-being?

In the tumultuous landscape of relationships affected by addiction, the adage "actions speak louder than words" takes on profound significance. It's easy to get caught up in the promises and reassurances of our loved ones struggling with addiction, but true insight often lies in their actions. In this context, "actions speak louder than words" emphasizes the importance of paying attention to the behavior of our loved ones, rather than solely relying on their words. While they may make promises of change or improvement, it's their consistent actions that ultimately reveal the truth of their intentions and commitment to recovery.

One effective way to gain clarity and insight into the dynamics of our relationships is by adopting a mindful approach to observation. This involves keeping notes on behaviors, patterns, and concerns that arise in our interactions with our loved ones. By keeping a record of observations, we create a tangible and objective means of tracking the reality of our relationship. This allows us to step back and assess the situation more objectively, rather than being swayed by emotions or wishful thinking. The act of tracking observations serves as a valuable tool for gaining insight and clarity. It allows us to identify recurring patterns, recognize triggers, and assess the impact of our loved one's behavior on our own well-being.

Through this process, we also cultivate a deeper understanding of which aspects of the relationship we can influence and those that are beyond our control. This discernment is essential for setting and maintaining boundaries that safeguard our mental health and well-being. By detaching emotionally from the situation, we create space to observe our loved one's behavior with greater objectivity. Removing the influence of emotion allows us to gain a clearer understanding of the dynamics at play and make more informed decisions about our next steps. As the saying goes, "It's hard to read the label when you're inside the jar." Shifting our perspective to that of an observer enables us to gain valuable insights that may have been obscured by our emotional involvement.

Prioritizing Truth: We Need to Love Truth More Than We Love Love

In navigating a relationship touched by addiction, it's essential to prioritize truth over the desire for love or validation. This means being willing to confront uncomfortable realities and acknowledge when our loved one's actions are not aligning with their words.

Loving Truth More Than Love. The phrase "we need to love truth more than we love love" encapsulates this idea. It reminds us that true love encompasses honesty, integrity, and authenticity. By prioritizing truth, even when it's painful or challenging, we empower ourselves to navigate our relationships with clarity and integrity.

In To Summarize, adopting a mindful approach to observing our loved one's actions, keeping notes, and prioritizing truth over love are essential strategies for gaining insight and clarity in relationships affected by addiction. By taking stock of the reality of our situations and detaching emotionally from the outcome, we empower ourselves to make informed decisions that pricritize our own well-being.

Cultivating Awareness: Recognizing the Impact of Abuse

If an observer, like a fly on the wall, were to witness the dynamics of your relationship, would they express concern? How do you imagine this hypothetical observer would perceive the interactions and behaviors within your relationship?

Let's gently explore the signs and effects of abuse within relationships impacted by addiction, fostering a compassionate understanding of these complex dynamics.

Recognizing Red Flags

It's important to acknowledge the warning signs that abuse may be present in a relationship. These signs can manifest in various forms, including physical, emotional, psychological, and sexual. Look for subtle cues such as manipulation, gaslighting, isolation, and controlling behaviors. Pay attention to your instincts and any feelings of discomfort or unease.

Recognizing red flags of abuse is crucial for safeguarding one's well-being in a relationship affected by addiction. Here's an elaboration on the different forms of abuse and their warning signs:

Physical Abuse: This involves any form of physical harm or violence inflicted upon an individual. Warning signs may include unexplained injuries, bruises, cuts, or broken bones. The abuser may also use physical force to intimidate or control the victim, leading to a fear of their safety.

Emotional Abuse: Emotional abuse is characterized by behaviors that undermine an individual's self-worth and emotional well-being. Warning signs include constant criticism, insults, humiliation, and belittling. The abuser may also use manipulation tactics to control the victim's thoughts, feelings, and actions.

Psychological Abuse: This form of abuse involves the use of psychological tactics to exert control and power over the victim. Warning signs may include gaslighting, where the abuser denies or distorts reality to make the victim doubt their perceptions and sanity. Other tactics may include threats, intimidation, and coercion.

Sexual Abuse: Sexual abuse encompasses any form of unwanted sexual contact or behavior imposed upon an individual without their consent. Warning signs may include coerced or forced sexual activity, sexual harassment, or exploitation. The abuser may manipulate or pressure the victim into engaging in sexual acts against their will.

Manipulation: Manipulation tactics are often used by abusers to exert control over their victims. This can include guilt-tripping, blame-shifting, or using emotional manipulation to manipulate the victim's behavior and decisions.

Gaslighting: Gaslighting is a form of psychological manipulation where the abuser undermines the victim's perception of reality. This can involve denying the victim's experiences, feelings, or memories, making them doubt their sanity and judgment.

Isolation: Abusers may isolate their victims from friends, family, and support networks as a means of exerting control. This can involve controlling their access to communication devices, monitoring their interactions, or preventing them from leaving the house without permission.

Controlling Behaviors: Controlling behaviors are often used by abusers to maintain power and dominance in the relationship. This can include monitoring the victim's movements, controlling their finances, or dictating their appearance and behavior.

By being aware of these warning signs and trusting your instincts, you can better protect yourself from potential abuse in a relationship affected by addiction. It's important to seek support from trusted friends, family members, or professionals if you recognize any of these red flags in your relationship.

Understanding the Impact on Your Well-being

Reflect: Take a moment to reflect on how your loved one's addiction is affecting you and your well-being. Consider the emotional toll it may be taking, as well as any changes in your behaviors or overall quality of life. Developing this awareness is a crucial step in recognizing the need for intervention and support.

Understanding the impact of your loved one's addiction on your own well-being is an essential aspect of navigating a relationship touched by addiction. Here's an elaboration on this concept.

Examples of Impact On Well-Being

Emotional Toll: Addiction can have a significant emotional impact on loved ones. Take a moment to reflect on your own emotional experiences, such as feelings of stress, anxiety, sadness, anger, or frustration. Consider how the unpredictability and instability of addiction may be affecting your mental and emotional state. It's important to acknowledge and validate your emotions, recognizing that they are a natural response to the challenges you are facing.

Changes in Behavior: Addiction can also lead to changes in behavior for both the individual struggling with addiction and their loved ones. Reflect on any shifts in your behavior patterns, such as increased stress levels, changes in sleep or eating habits, withdrawal from social activities, or engaging in unhealthy coping mechanisms. These changes may be indicative of the impact that addiction is having on your overall well-being.

Quality of Life: Consider how addiction is influencing your overall quality of life. Are you experiencing disruptions in your daily routine or responsibilities? Are you struggling to maintain relationships or fulfill your personal goals and aspirations? Reflect on any areas of your life that have been negatively impacted by addiction, whether it's your career, finances, physical health, or social connections.

Developing awareness of these aspects is a crucial first step in recognizing the need for intervention and support. By acknowledging the impact of addiction on your own well-being, you empower yourself to take proactive steps towards self-care and seek out the necessary resources and assistance. Whether it's reaching out to a support group, seeking therapy, or setting boundaries in your relationship, prioritizing your own well-being is essential for navigating the complexities of a relationship affected by addiction.

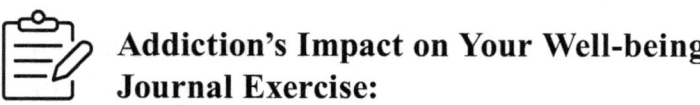 **Addiction's Impact on Your Well-being Journal Exercise:**

Take some time to journal or reflect on the following questions:

- How do I feel in my relationship with my addicted loved one?

- Have I noticed any patterns of behavior that may be indicative of abuse?

- How has addiction impacted my emotions, behaviors, and overall well-being?

- Am I experiencing feelings of manipulation, isolation, or control in my relationship?

By engaging in this exercise, you can deepen your understanding of the dynamics at play and begin to identify areas where support may be needed. Remember, you are not alone, and there are resources available to help you navigate these challenging circumstances with compassion and resilience.

Breaking the Cycle: Healing from Trauma and Ending Abusive Patterns:

Understanding Trauma

Trauma comes in various forms, ranging from significant life-altering events (big T trauma) to chronic, less obvious stressors (little t trauma). Both types of trauma can have a profound impact on our well-being, influencing our thoughts, emotions, and behaviors. Big T trauma may include experiences like physical or sexual abuse, natural disasters, or accidents, while little t trauma can encompass ongoing stressors such as neglect, emotional abuse, or witnessing domestic violence. Recognizing the effects of trauma on our lives is essential for understanding its role in shaping our responses to addiction and abuse.

Trauma Bonds

Trauma bonding is a phenomenon commonly observed in relationships affected by addiction, where individuals form strong emotional attachments to their abusers despite experiencing harm or mistreatment. This bond often develops due to a combination of factors, including intermittent reinforcement and perceived acts of kindness from the abuser.

In the context of addiction, the unpredictable nature of the addict's behavior can create a cycle of highs and lows in the relationship. During periods of sobriety or remorse, the addicted individual may exhibit moments of affection, remorse, or promises of change, which can lead their loved ones to feel hopeful and emotionally connected. However, these moments are often short-lived and followed by relapse or abusive behavior, leading to confusion and emotional turmoil for the victim.

Additionally, trauma bonding can be reinforced by feelings of love, loyalty, and dependency that develop over time in the relationship. Many individuals may struggle to reconcile the negative aspects of their partner's behavior with the positive qualities they once admired, leading to a sense of cognitive dissonance and internal conflict.

Furthermore, fear often plays a significant role in trauma bonding, as victims may worry about the consequences of leaving the relationship or fear retaliation from their abuser. This fear, combined with feelings of shame, guilt, and isolation, can create a powerful psychological barrier that prevents individuals from seeking help or leaving the abusive situation.

Breaking free from trauma bonds requires courage, self-awareness, and support from trusted individuals and professionals. It involves recognizing the unhealthy dynamics at play in the relationship, setting boundaries, and prioritizing one's well-being. By seeking therapy or counseling, attending support groups, and accessing community resources, individuals can begin to untangle themselves from the grip of trauma bonding and pave the way for healing and empowerment.

Breaking Free From Trauma Bonds

Breaking free from trauma bonds requires a combination of self-awareness, courage, and support. Here are some steps that can help in breaking trauma bonds:

Recognize the Bond: The first step is acknowledging that a trauma bond exists in the relationship. This involves recognizing the unhealthy patterns of behavior, manipulation, and abuse, and understanding how they have influenced your feelings and actions.

Seek Support: Reach out to trusted friends, family members, or professionals who can provide support and guidance. Talking to someone who understands your situation can offer validation, perspective, and encouragement.

Educate Yourself: Learn about trauma bonding and the dynamics of abusive relationships. Understanding the psychological mechanisms at play can help you recognize and challenge distorted thoughts and beliefs.

Set Boundaries: Establish clear boundaries with the abusive individual to protect yourself from further harm. This may involve limiting contact, refusing to engage in manipulative behavior, and prioritizing your own well-being.

Practice Self-Care: Take care of yourself physically, emotionally, and mentally. Engage in activities that bring you joy and fulfillment, and prioritize your health and happiness.

Challenge Distorted Beliefs: Identify and challenge any beliefs or thoughts that reinforce the trauma bond. This may involve questioning beliefs about love, loyalty, and self-worth, and replacing them with more realistic and empowering beliefs.

Seek Professional Help: Consider seeking therapy or counseling to work through your experiences, process your emotions, and develop coping strategies. A qualified therapist can provide support, guidance, and tools for healing.

Create a Safety Plan: If you are in immediate danger or fear for your safety, create a safety plan to protect yourself and your loved ones. This may involve identifying safe places to go, having emergency contacts, and accessing resources such as hotlines or shelters.

Focus on Healing: Healing from trauma bonds takes time and effort, so be patient and compassionate with yourself. Focus on healing and rebuilding your life, and surround yourself with people who support and uplift you.

Breaking trauma bonds is a challenging and often painful process, but it is essential for reclaiming your autonomy, well-being, and sense of self. With support, courage, and determination, you can break free from the grip of trauma bonds and create a life filled with safety, empowerment, and healing.

Understanding the Drama Triangle

The drama triangle is a psychological model that describes three roles often present in dysfunctional relationships: the victim, the persecutor, and the rescuer. These roles can perpetuate abusive patterns and undermine healthy communication and boundaries. Empowering yourself involves stepping out of these roles and reclaiming agency and autonomy in your relationships. By recognizing when you're caught in the drama triangle and taking proactive steps to assert your boundaries and needs, you can break free from the cycle of abuse and create healthier dynamics.

In the context of loving someone with an addiction, the drama triangle can manifest in various ways. The individual struggling with addiction may initially take on the role of the victim, portraying themselves as helpless or powerless in the face of their addiction. As a result, their loved ones may unconsciously adopt the role of the rescuer, believing that they can save or fix the person with addiction.

Conversely, the individual with addiction may also play the role of the persecutor, blaming others for their struggles or lashing out in anger or frustration. In response, their loved ones may feel like victims, experiencing guilt, shame, or fear as a result of the addiction's impact on their lives.

The drama triangle can create a cycle of dysfunction and enable unhealthy patterns to persist. The rescuer may feel a sense of obligation or responsibility to continue enabling the person with addiction, while the victim may feel trapped in a cycle of abuse and manipulation.

Empowering yourself involves recognizing when you're caught in the drama triangle and actively choosing to step out of these roles. This may involve setting clear boundaries, practicing self-care, and prioritizing your own well-being. By asserting your needs and boundaries, you can break free from the cycle of abuse and create healthier dynamics in your relationships.

Breaking the Cycle

Breaking free from the cycle of abuse and trauma necessitates courage, self-awareness, and a supportive network. Prioritizing your well-being, seek guidance from trusted individuals and professionals who can provide resources and assistance. Effective strategies may involve therapy, support groups, safety planning, and accessing community resources. By proactively addressing trauma and establishing boundaries, you lay the groundwork for healing, personal growth, and empowerment within your relationships.

Empowerment emerges through heightened awareness of unhealthy dynamics. This awareness signifies a commitment to recognizing and confronting uncomfortable truths. By shining a light on these patterns, you reclaim control over your emotional well-being and create opportunities for positive transformation.

The journey begins with recognition—a crucial step towards dismantling destructive patterns. Listen to your intuition, acknowledging the impact of certain behaviors on your mental and emotional state. Recognize moments where boundaries are violated, feelings are disregarded, or your sense of self is compromised.

Empowering change involves setting firm boundaries that protect your emotional health and holding both yourself and others accountable for cultivating a nurturing, respectful environment. As you unveil these destructive patterns, you create space for growth, understanding, and healing. Remember, acknowledging these dynamics is not an admission of failure but a courageous stride towards reclaiming autonomy and fostering relationships that foster mutual empowerment and well-being.

In the forthcoming chapter, we will delve deeper into the pivotal role of boundaries in navigating relationships affected by addiction and abuse. Whether you choose to stay, leave, or find a middle ground, empowering yourself with the ability to set boundaries is essential. Boundaries serve as crucial safeguards for our well-being, providing clarity and protection amidst the complexities of these relationships. We will explore the intricacies of setting and maintaining healthy boundaries, recognizing them not as barriers to connection but as frameworks for fostering respect, safety, and autonomy. By honing our boundary-setting skills, we empower ourselves to assert our needs, safeguard our emotional space, and gain clarity on the direction of our relationships.

To Summarize

Understanding abuse, trauma, and unhealthy dynamics is crucial when navigating tough decisions about whether to stay or leave a relationship, particularly one affected by addiction. This awareness provides clarity about the impact of the relationship on your well-being, helping you recognize red flags, set boundaries, and prioritize your own safety and emotional health. By acknowledging the presence of abuse and trauma, you empower yourself to make informed decisions that align with your values and needs. Additionally, this awareness enables you to see beyond the facade of addiction and understand the underlying dynamics at play, such as trauma bonding and the cycle of abuse. Armed with this understanding, you can approach the decision-making process with compassion for yourself and a clear-eyed assessment of the relationship's potential for growth or toxicity.

Key Insights

Understanding the Intersection of Addiction and Abuse: In relationships affected by addiction, toxic dynamics can thrive, often hidden by the complexities of addiction. Unveiling these patterns is essential to reclaiming personal strength and well-being, fostering connections rooted in respect and vitality.

Recognizing Signs and Effects of Abuse: Abuse, in its various forms, aims to exert power and control, resulting in harm or distress. Recognizing these signs is crucial for promoting safety and prioritizing our well-being in relationships.

Breaking Trauma Bonds: In relationships affected by addiction, trauma bonds can form, tying individuals to their abusers despite harm. Breaking free requires courage, self-awareness, and support to untangle oneself and pave the way for healing.

Consolidating Our Insights: Recognizing abusive and unhealthy dynamics in our relationships can significantly aid us in navigating tough relationship decisions. By unmasking abusive behavior and acknowledging unhealthy patterns, we gain clarity and insight into the true nature of our relationships. This awareness empowers us to make informed choices about whether to stay or go, prioritizing our well-being and safety.

Moreover, cultivating awareness of the impacts of addiction further enhances our ability to navigate relationship decisions. Understanding how addiction affects dynamics such as trust, communication, and emotional stability helps us gain clarity and perspective on the challenges we face. Breaking the cycle's of abuse and recognizing trauma and trauma bonds also play a crucial role in our decision-making process. By acknowledging the cycle of abuse and trauma in our relationships, we can begin the healing process and move towards healthier dynamics.

The concept of a bruised heart, symbolizing the emotional toll of abusive and unhealthy relationships, underscores the importance of unmasking these issues. By shining a light on the hidden wounds and scars, we empower ourselves to prioritize our well-being and make decisions aligned with our values and needs.

Overall, these insights contribute to our enlightenment and self-discovery by guiding us to understand our own boundaries, values, and priorities. This self-awareness and clarity enable us to navigate tough relationship decisions with confidence and resilience, supported by the love and compassion of those around us.

Reflection: *As you reflect on the insights shared about recognizing abusive and unhealthy dynamics in relationships, consider the following: How has becoming aware of these patterns empowered you to navigate tough relationship decisions? What steps can you take to unmask abusive behavior and acknowledge unhealthy patterns in your own relationships? How do you envision prioritizing your well-being and safety as you make informed choices about whether to stay or go?*

CHAPTER 5

CROSSING THE LINE

Navigating Boundaries, Ultimatums, and Rules for Love

Introduction

In this chapter, we go on an exploration of the indispensable role that boundaries play in navigating relationships affected by addiction. Rather than viewing boundaries as restrictive barriers, we'll adopt a fresh perspective, framing them as personal guidelines or affirmations of self-care – essentially, what we're saying "yes" to in our lives. This journey is about understanding how boundaries serve us, allowing us to prioritize our own emotional and mental well-being. It is my hope that you see boundaries in a whole new light.

It's a delicate balance between love and self-preservation, understanding and asserting boundaries, and effective communication amidst turmoil. Whether you're contemplating staying or leaving, safeguarding your well-being remains paramount. We'll uncover the significance of prioritizing our own needs and establishing boundaries, which are essentially your own personal rules to live by, that honor our emotional and mental health.

Through engaging reflective exercises, we'll pinpoint the behaviors and situations we're willing to tolerate and those that unequivocally cross our boundaries. We'll distinguish between what we have control over and what we do not, recognizing that our boundaries are about how we react for our own self-preservation, rather than trying to change or control others.

Central to effective boundary-setting is communication. We'll delve into non-violent communication techniques designed to navigate challenging conversations with empathy and self-compassion, helping us express our needs while fostering deeper connections and mutual respect.

Armed with a keen awareness of our limits and an unwavering commitment to authenticity, we'll find clarity and empowerment in our decision-making process. Together, let's embrace the journey of defining our path in love, anchored by resilient boundaries for self-preservation and the freedom to prioritize our well-being above all else.

Have you ever reached a point where you've exclaimed, 'Enough is enough! I can't handle this anymore. This has become ridiculous.' Has there been a moment when you felt someone has crossed the line?

Regardless of Staying or Going: Protecting Your Well-being

Navigating relationships affected by addiction can be a challenging and often confusing journey, especially when it comes to understanding and implementing boundaries. Boundaries, in essence, are personal guidelines or rules to live by that safeguard our well-being. However, they are frequently misunderstood and can seem overwhelming or elusive.

To demystify boundaries, it's essential to adopt a new perspective, one that centers entirely on you. Rather than viewing boundaries as restrictive barriers or attempts to control others, consider them as affirmations of self-care and empowerment. Think of boundaries as the positive actions you take to define what you will and will not tolerate in your life, essentially what you are saying "yes" to. Boundaries are about what you desire for yourself and your own well-being.

Approaching boundaries in this light is profoundly empowering. It shifts the focus from trying to change or control someone else's behavior to prioritizing your own needs and values. Boundaries become a reflection of your self-worth and a means of safeguarding your emotional and mental well-being.

It's crucial to recognize that boundaries are completely about you, not your addicted loved one. While it's natural to want to influence their behavior or protect them from harm, the reality is that we cannot control others. This concept, known as the locus of control, underscores the importance of setting boundaries for ourselves and not for others.

Here are some examples of boundaries that are about personal rules to live by and guidelines for your own well-being:

Emotional Boundaries:
I will not engage in conversations that make me feel belittled or invalidated.

I will not tolerate being yelled at or spoken to disrespectfully.

I will take time for myself to process my emotions before responding to conflict.

I will prioritize self-care activities such as meditation, journaling, or spending time in nature to nurture my emotional well-being.

Physical Boundaries:
I will maintain a healthy work-life balance and prioritize adequate rest and sleep.

I will prioritize regular exercise and physical activity to keep my body healthy and strong.

I will not engage in any sexual activity that I am not comfortable with or that compromises my physical health.

I will respect my body's signals and take breaks when I feel tired or overwhelmed.

Social Boundaries:
I will spend time with people who uplift and support me, and distance myself from those who drain my energy or bring negativity into my life.

I will set limits on how much time I spend on social media or with toxic individuals who do not respect my boundaries.

I will prioritize quality time with loved ones and set aside time for meaningful connections and relationships.

I will not tolerate gossip or negative talk about others in my social circles.

Time Boundaries:
I will set aside dedicated time for work, leisure, and relaxation to maintain a healthy balance in my life.

I will say no to commitments or obligations that do not align with my priorities or values.

I will communicate my boundaries around time management to others and assertively decline requests that interfere with my schedule.

I will prioritize activities and hobbies that bring me joy and fulfillment, even if it means saying no to other obligations.

Financial Boundaries:
I will create and stick to a budget that aligns with my financial goals and priorities.

I will not lend money to others if it compromises my own financial stability or well-being.

I will communicate my financial boundaries clearly to friends and family members and refrain from feeling guilty about saying no to requests for money.

I will prioritize saving and investing in my future while also enjoying present moments within my means.

These examples illustrate how boundaries can serve as personal guidelines and rules to live by, helping to safeguard your well-being in various aspects of life.

Here's an exercise to help you identify your values, needs, and wants, and then formulate them into personal boundaries or rules to live by:

 ## Creating Your Personal Boundaries Declaration Exercise

Reflect on Your Values
Take some time to reflect on what matters most to you in life. Consider the principles and beliefs that guide your decisions and actions. Write down a list of your core values, such as honesty, respect, compassion, integrity, freedom, etc.

Identify Your Needs and Wants
Think about your emotional, physical, social, and financial needs, as well as your desires and aspirations. Consider what you require to feel fulfilled, happy, and balanced in different areas of your life. Make a list of your needs and wants, both practical and emotional.

Formulate Your Personal Boundaries
Based on your values, needs, and wants, begin to formulate your personal boundaries or rules to live by. These boundaries should serve as guidelines for how you interact with others and how you prioritize your own well-being. Use the following format to create your boundaries declaration.

"I value [value], and therefore, I will [action] to honor that value. My needs and wants include [needs/wants], so I will [action] to fulfill them. In order to safeguard my well-being and happiness, I establish the following personal boundaries:

- _____

CHAPTER 5: CROSSING THE LINE

- _____

- _____

[Additional Boundaries as needed]

Write Your Personal Boundaries Declaration
Use the format provided above to craft your own personal boundaries declaration. Be specific and clear about what behaviors and situations you will and will not tolerate in your life. Consider different areas such as relationships, work, health, and personal growth.

Review and Refine Your Declaration
Once you've written your personal boundaries declaration, take some time to review it and make any necessary revisions. Ensure that your boundaries align with your values, needs, and wants, and that they reflect your commitment to prioritizing your well-being.

Declare Your Boundaries
Finally, declare your boundaries to yourself and, if appropriate, share them with trusted friends, family members, or partners. Communicate your boundaries assertively and confidently, and be prepared to uphold them in your interactions and relationships.

By completing this exercise, you'll gain clarity on your values, needs, and wants, and you'll establish clear boundaries to protect your well-being and happiness in various aspects of your life.

By understanding and implementing boundaries effectively, you gain clarity on your values and boundaries, making it easier to navigate tough relationship. Boundaries serve as guiding principles, signaling when to stay, when to leave, or when to find a middle ground in a relationship affected by addiction all while safeguarding your well-being They empower you to make choices aligned with your well-being and happiness, regardless of the path you choose.

Navigating Boundaries: Understanding Ultimatums and Imposed Boundaries in Relationships

Have you ever felt so overwhelmed by your loved one's addiction that you resorted to issuing a threat or ultimatum, like saying 'If you do that one more time, I'm out'?

Feeling out of control is a common experience when loving someone struggling with addiction. The sheer weight of helplessness can drive us to desperate measures, including resorting to threats and ultimatums in a last-ditch effort to make an impact. However, as we'll explore in this section, ultimatums and imposed boundaries often fail to produce lasting change in relationships affected by addiction.

At the breaking point, when sacrifices of personal happiness become unsustainable, the phrase "You've Crossed The Line: Enough Is Enough" marks a pivotal moment. This moment signifies the realization that prioritizing one's well-being is imperative, even if it means making difficult decisions about the future of the relationship.

Despite our best intentions, we sometimes confuse boundary-setting with attempts to control others. This misunderstanding can lead us to impose rules on our loved ones, believing that it will influence their behavior. However, boundaries are not about controlling others; they are about defining what behaviors and situations align with our values and well-being.

For example, setting a boundary like "You can't do drugs in the house" may seem reasonable, but it overlooks the fundamental truth that we cannot control another person's actions. Instead, effective boundaries focus on our own actions and well-being. Shifting to a boundary like "If I am ever exposed to or see any drugs in the house, I will immediately remove myself" prioritizes self-preservation over attempting to control someone else's behavior.

Ultimatum: An ultimatum is a final, uncompromising demand or set of terms issued by one party to another, typically with the threat of a negative consequence if the terms are not met. It is a statement of "do this, or else." Ultimatums are often used as a way to exert control or influence over someone's behavior or decision-making. In relationships, ultimatums are usually issued when one person feels frustrated, powerless, or at a breaking point. However, they can be counterproductive and may lead to resentment, defiance, or further conflict rather than producing the desired change. Ultimatums are different from setting boundaries, as boundaries are about asserting one's needs and values without coercing or manipulating others.

It's crucial to differentiate between boundaries and attempts to control or manipulate others. Boundaries serve as guidelines for asserting our needs and values, empowering us to prioritize our well-being within our relationships.

Imposed Boundaries: Imposed boundaries refer to boundaries that are set by one person onto another, often without mutual agreement or understanding. These boundaries are typically established with the intention of controlling or regulating the behavior of the other person, rather than being mutually respected guidelines for both individuals. Imposed boundaries can arise from a variety of circumstances, such as power imbalances in relationships, attempts to influence or control others, or a lack of communication and understanding. In the context of relationships affected by addiction, imposed boundaries may be attempted as a way to address problematic behavior, but they can often lead to conflict, resentment, and further deterioration of the relationship. It's important to differentiate between imposed boundaries and healthy, personal boundaries that prioritize the your well-being and the autonomy of both individuals involved.

Ultimately, imposing boundaries onto others is futile for several reasons. Firstly, we cannot control someone else's behavior, especially when it comes to addiction. Secondly, threats and ultimatums can create unhealthy dynamics in relationships, eroding trust and exacerbating struggles with addiction. Lastly, threats and ultimatums ignore personal boundaries, focusing on changing someone else's behavior rather than honoring our own limits and needs.

Accepting Limits: Understanding the Boundaries of Influence in Relationships

We don't have control over another human being, especially when it comes to addiction, primarily because addiction itself entails a loss of control over one's behavior. Addiction is a complex condition characterized by compulsive substance use or behavior despite harmful consequences. Individuals struggling with addiction often find it challenging to control their impulses, cravings, and actions, even if they recognize the negative impact it has on their lives and relationships.

Moreover, addiction affects the brain's functioning, particularly areas related to decision-making, impulse control, and judgment. As a result, individuals with addiction may engage in behaviors that are harmful to themselves and others, even when they desire to change or stop.

Instead of trying to control someone else's behavior, it's more productive to focus on setting boundaries for ourselves, prioritizing our well-being, and encouraging our loved ones to seek help and support for their addiction from qualified professionals. This approach fosters empathy, understanding, and collaboration, which are essential components of supporting someone through their recovery journey.

It's crucial to differentiate between boundaries and attempts to control or manipulate others. Boundaries serve as guidelines for asserting your needs and values, not as means of coercion or punishment. By understanding and implementing boundaries effectively, we create a space of empowerment and self-care within our relationships. Now, let's delve into why approaches such as threatening, punishing, or ultimatums in boundary setting ultimately prove ineffective.

Responses to Helplessness: Navigating Boundaries and Ultimatums in the Face of Addiction

Feeling helpless when dealing with a loved one's addiction is a deeply human response, rooted in a desire to alleviate their suffering and restore balance to the relationship. Addiction often brings chaos, instability, and pain into the lives of both the individual struggling with it and their loved ones. Witnessing someone we care about spiral into destructive behaviors despite our efforts to help can evoke feelings of frustration, fear, sadness, and powerlessness.

In the face of such overwhelming emotions, it's understandable that we may resort to imposing boundaries, giving threats, or ultimatums as a last resort. These actions are often driven by a desperate need to regain some sense of control over the situation and protect our own well-being. We may hope that by setting firm boundaries or issuing ultimatums, we can compel our loved one to recognize the severity of their addiction and seek help.

Moreover, the urgency of the situation and the fear of witnessing further harm or loss can intensify our inclination to take drastic measures. We may believe that imposing consequences or issuing ultimatums will finally prompt our loved one to confront their addiction and make positive changes.

However, it's essential to approach these actions with compassion and self-awareness. While they may stem from a place of genuine concern and a desire to help, ultimatums and threats often come from a mindset of coercion and control, which can strain relationships and exacerbate feelings of shame and guilt in the individual struggling with addiction.

Instead of resorting to ultimatums or threats, it's crucial to recognize the limitations of our influence and focus on supporting our loved one with empathy, understanding, and encouragement. By cultivating a compassionate and non-judgmental attitude, we can create an environment conducive to open communication, trust, and healing, which are essential components of the recovery process. Additionally, seeking guidance from addiction professionals and support groups can provide us with the tools and resources needed to navigate the complexities of addiction while prioritizing our own well-being.

Navigating Boundaries and Breaking Points

In relationships affected by addiction, it's common to experience a sense of helplessness and frustration. Loving someone who struggles with addiction often leaves us feeling out of control, as we witness their behavior spiral and our efforts to help them seem futile. This feeling of powerlessness can lead us to a breaking point, where we're compelled to take drastic measures in an attempt to regain some sense of control.

At these breaking points, we may resort to ultimatums, threats, or attempts to control the behavior of our loved ones. However, these actions typically stem from a place of desperation rather than empowerment. They signify that our limits have been reached, and we're doing our best to make an impact in a situation that feels overwhelming and unmanageable.

Recognizing when someone has crossed the line is crucial in determining the future of the relationship. It's a moment of clarity where we acknowledge that sacrificing our happiness for someone who is unwilling to help themselves is no longer sustainable. This awareness can guide us in making difficult decisions about whether to stay in the relationship or walk away.

Two Key Aspects of Boundaries

First, establishing personal boundaries or rules to live by is crucial for self-care while navigating relationships impacted by addiction. These boundaries serve as guidelines for taking good care of our mental health, providing self-care and prioritizing our well-being.

Secondly, it's important to recognize your personal limits, knowing when you've been pushed to your breaking point. This involves understanding when certain behaviors or situations become intolerable or compromise your emotional well-being. Recognizing these limits allows you to assert yourself and take necessary steps to protect your mental health and overall well-being.

As a reminder, it's important to establish boundaries that prioritize our well-being and to differentiate between setting personal boundaries and the ability to know your limits. Setting personal boundaries can be a fun and uplifting process that allows us to assert our needs and values while maintaining a sense of autonomy and self-respect. Understanding your limits can be incredibly empowering, as it grants you a sense of control and heightened awareness to recognize when boundaries have been crossed. This awareness enables you to assertively safeguard your well-being and take appropriate action when necessary.

Understanding your limits is crucial for maintaining your emotional well-being and preserving healthy relationships.

Here's why knowing your limits is so important

Self-awareness: Knowing your limits requires self-awareness and introspection. It involves understanding your emotions, needs, and boundaries in various situations. When you know your limits, you're better equipped to recognize when something doesn't feel right or when you're being pushed beyond your comfort zone.

Boundary Setting: Knowing your limits enables you to establish and maintain healthy boundaries in your relationships. Boundaries define what is acceptable and unacceptable behavior for you, and they serve as a guide for how others should treat you. By being aware of your limits, you can communicate your boundaries effectively and assertively.

Self-Respect: Understanding your limits is an act of self-respect. It means valuing yourself enough to recognize when you're being mistreated or when your needs are not being met. When you honor your limits, you send a message to yourself and others that you deserve to be treated with kindness, respect, and consideration.

Empowerment: Knowing your limits empowers you to make choices that align with your values and priorities. It gives you the confidence to advocate for yourself and assert your needs in your relationships. When you're aware of your limits, you're less likely to tolerate behavior that undermines your well-being or compromises your values.

Healthy Relationships: Understanding your limits is essential for fostering healthy and fulfilling relationships. It allows you to set realistic expectations for yourself and others, which contributes to mutual respect and understanding. When both parties are aware of and respect each other's limits, conflicts are less likely to arise, and the relationship can thrive.

To help you identify your limits and set effective boundaries, try the following exercise:

Defining Your Limits Line In The Sand Boundaries Exercise

Reflect on Your Values and Needs: Take a moment to think about what matters most to you in your relationships. Consider your core values and the things you need to feel fulfilled and respected.

Recall Past Experiences: Think back on past experiences where you felt uncomfortable or overwhelmed in a relationship. Identify specific instances where your boundaries were crossed or you felt that your well-being was compromised.

Identify Boundary-Crossing Behaviors: Determine the behaviors or situations that have made you feel uncomfortable or compromised in the past. These could include actions or words from your partner or loved one that made you feel disrespected or undervalued.

Draw Your Line in the Sand: Define where your limits lie. Consider what behaviors or actions are unacceptable to you and where you draw the line in your relationships. This is about recognizing when something crosses the line for you personally.

Create Personal Boundaries: Based on your reflections, create a list of personal boundaries or rules to live by that align with your values and prioritize your well-being. These boundaries should serve as guidelines for how you take good care of yourself. This personal boundaries are meant to empower you and safe-guard your well-being.

Make a Commitment to Yourself: Make a vow to yourself to assert these boundaries assertively and consistently in your relationships. Practice communicating your boundaries with confidence, knowing that you deserve to be treated with respect and compassion.

Empower Yourself: By knowing your limits and setting clear personal boundaries, you empower yourself to navigate relationships affected by addiction with confidence and resilience. Remember that you have the right to prioritize your well-being and establish boundaries that honor your needs and values.

Overall, knowing your limits is essential for maintaining emotional balance, preserving self-respect, and nurturing healthy relationships.

It enables you to navigate life's challenges with confidence and resilience, ensuring that your well-being remains a top priority.

Empowered Decision-Making

Decision-making is the process of selecting the best course of action from among multiple alternatives. It involves evaluating various factors, weighing pros and cons, and ultimately choosing the option that aligns with one's goals, values, and priorities.

Knowing your limits is a crucial aspect of decision-making, particularly in relationships affected by addiction. Here's why:

Clarity and Self-Awareness: Understanding your limits helps you gain clarity about what you are and are not willing to tolerate in your relationships. It enables you to recognize behaviors or situations that compromise your well-being and identify when your boundaries have been crossed.

Informed Choices: When you know your limits, you can make more informed choices about how to respond to challenging situations. For example, if you have clearly defined boundaries regarding substance abuse in your relationship, you can make decisions about whether to stay, leave, or seek outside support based on those boundaries.

Empowerment: Knowing your limits empowers you to advocate for yourself and assert your needs in your relationships. It gives you the confidence to communicate your boundaries effectively and take action to protect your well-being when necessary.

Conflict Resolution: Understanding your limits can help facilitate conflict resolution by providing clarity on what is acceptable to you and what is not. It allows you to express your boundaries assertively and work towards finding mutually acceptable solutions with your partner.

Setting Goals and Priorities: Knowing your limits allows you to set clear goals and priorities for yourself in your relationships. It helps you prioritize your well-being and focus on what truly matters to you, guiding your decision-making process accordingly.

To Summarize, knowing your limits is an essential component of effective decision-making in relationships affected by addiction. It provides a foundation of self-awareness, empowerment, and clarity that enables you to navigate challenges, advocate for yourself, and make choices that align with your values and priorities.

Recognizing the significance of knowing your limits is pivotal in making informed decisions about the future of your relationship. You may find yourself doing all that you know, trying everything to safeguard your mental health and well-being, regardless of how your efforts are met. This awareness is a testament to your commitment to prioritizing yourself amidst the challenges of a relationship affected by addiction.

Self-awareness and boundary-setting play critical roles in this process, contributing to clarity and empowerment in decision-making. By understanding your own needs, feelings, and limits, you gain valuable insights into what is and isn't acceptable to you. Establishing clear boundaries reinforces your commitment to self-care and ensures that your well-being remains a top priority.

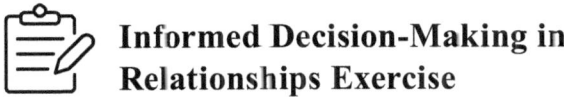 ## Informed Decision-Making in Relationships Exercise

In relationships affected by addiction, understanding your limits is crucial for making informed decisions and maintaining your well-being. This exercise will guide you through a process of self-discovery to identify and explore your personal limits, empowering you to make decisions that align with your values and priorities.

Instructions

Reflect on Past Decision-Making
Take some time to reflect on past decisions you've made in your relationship with your addicted loved one. Consider moments when you felt uncertain, conflicted, or overwhelmed. What factors influenced your decisions? How did you feel before and after making them?

Identify Decision-Making Triggers
Think about specific situations or challenges that trigger difficult decision-making processes. These triggers could include instances of relapse, dishonesty, conflict, or boundary violations. Write down the triggers that make decision-making challenging for you.

Clarify Your Values and Priorities
Reflect on your values and priorities in relationships. What are the most important aspects of a healthy relationship to you? Examples may include trust, respect, communication, and personal well-being. Consider how these values inform your decision-making process.

Define Your Decision-Making Boundaries
Based on your reflections, begin to define your decision-making boundaries. These boundaries represent the limits of what you are willing to tolerate or accept in your relationship. Be specific about behaviors, actions, and situations that impact your decision-making.

Consider Physical, Emotional, and Mental Limits
Explore your physical, emotional, and mental limits in the context of decision-making. Physical limits may involve safety concerns or instances of harm. Emotional and mental limits may relate to stress, anxiety, or feelings of being overwhelmed.

Evaluate Your Comfort Zones
Assess your comfort zones in the decision-making process. Where do you feel confident and empowered to make decisions? Where do you feel uncertain or hesitant? Recognize that it's okay to seek support or guidance when making difficult decisions.

Practice Informed Decision-Making
Practice informed decision-making by considering the potential consequences and outcomes of your choices. Think about how your decisions align with your values, priorities, and boundaries. Use journaling or visualization techniques to explore different scenarios and outcomes.

Reflect on Your Decision-Making Process
Reflect on your decision-making process and any insights you've gained. Celebrate moments where you've made decisions that honor your well-being and values. Acknowledge any challenges or areas for growth. Remember that decision-making is a skill that improves with practice and self-awareness.

Understanding your limits is a powerful tool for making informed decisions in relationships affected by addiction. By exploring your boundaries, clarifying your values, and practicing informed decision-making, you empower yourself to navigate challenges and prioritize your well-being.

Empowering Communication: Navigating Boundaries with Nonviolent Communication

Amidst the complexities of relationships entangled in addiction, establishing boundaries is crucial, but so too is our capacity to articulate and communicate those boundaries. When we're in the heat of the moment, feeling angry or overtaken by emotions, it's hard not to resort to blaming, threatening, or giving ultimatums. Yet, we know that these strategies ultimately don't work. However, there is a communication style that is effective in preserving your mental health and has shown to have a great impact on relationships.

In relationships, effective communication is the cornerstone of establishing and maintaining boundaries, especially in contexts affected by addiction. Nonviolent Communication (NVC) offers a framework for clearer communication, self-awareness, and boundary-setting, which is essential for fostering healthier relationships.

In these challenging moments, effective communication becomes essential. While our efforts to convey boundaries may not always be met with the same level of respect, it serves as a vital tool for ensuring our needs are potentially acknowledged and addressed. Even if it's just for our own sake of clarity and understanding. By utilizing strategies like Nonviolent Communication (NVC), pioneered by Marshall

Rosenberg, we can navigate these difficult conversations with greater clarity and compassion.

Understanding the Role of Effective Communication

Effective communication serves as the bedrock for setting and upholding boundaries in relationships. It fosters mutual understanding, respect, and cooperation between individuals.

Assertive communication enables individuals to express their needs and boundaries without resorting to blame or manipulation.

Nonviolent Communication (NVC) is highly effective in relationships and for safeguarding our well-being due to several key reasons:

Emphasis on Empathy: NVC prioritizes empathy, both towards oneself and others. By fostering understanding and compassion, it promotes healthier interactions and reduces conflict. When we empathize with others' feelings and needs, we create a supportive environment where mutual respect thrives.

Clarity and Self-awareness: NVC encourages individuals to identify and express their emotions, needs, and values clearly and authentically. This clarity fosters self-awareness, enabling individuals to recognize their boundaries and assert them confidently. When we are in tune with our own needs and values, we are better equipped to communicate them effectively to others.

Nonjudgmental Communication: Nonviolent Communication (NVC) facilitates nonjudgmental communication, creating a safe space for individuals to express themselves without fear of criticism or rejection. This open and accepting approach fosters trust and honesty, paving the way for deeper connections and understanding in relationships. It serves as a valuable tool, particularly in challenging or emotionally charged situations, enabling individuals to calmly assess their thoughts and feelings.

Important Note About NVC: However, it's important to acknowledge that the same level of NVC may not always be reciprocated, especially in the context of addiction. Despite this limitation, practicing NVC remains empowering, offering greater clarity about the dynamics at play and helping individuals navigate complex emotions and interactions with resilience. By embracing NVC principles, individuals can assert their needs and values confidently, fostering healthier and more authentic relationships, even in the face of adversity.

Conflict Resolution: NVC provides practical tools for resolving conflicts peacefully and constructively. By focusing on underlying needs rather than positions or demands, it helps individuals find mutually satisfactory solutions. This collaborative approach can reduce tension and promotes the chances of a win-win outcome, enhancing well-being.

Resilience In Challenging Situations: In relationships affected by addiction or other complex issues, NVC equips individuals with the skills to navigate difficult emotions and conversations with resilience. By staying connected to their own needs and values, individuals can maintain a sense of inner strength and clarity, even in challenging circumstances.

Overall, NVC empowers you to communicate assertively, empathize with others, and prioritize your well-being in relationships. By fostering understanding, respect, and authenticity, it lays the foundation for healthier and more fulfilling connections with others while preserving your well-being.

Step-by-Step Guide to Effective Communication and Conflict Resolution

The Nonviolent Communication (NVC) model is a powerful framework for effective communication and conflict resolution. It consists of four key components: Observation, Feeling, Need, and Request (or Action).

Here's a step-by-step guide on how to use each component of NVC:

Observation:
- Start by objectively observing the situation or behavior without judgment or evaluation.

- Describe what you see or hear, focusing on concrete, observable facts rather than interpretations or assumptions.

- Use language that is specific, clear, and non-blaming.

- Avoid labeling or interpreting the other person's behavior. Stick to describing the facts as they are.

Feeling:
- Identify and express your feelings in response to the observed situation or behavior.

- Be honest and authentic about your emotions without placing blame or judgment on yourself or others.

- Use "I" statements to take ownership of your feelings. For example, instead of saying, "You make me feel..." say, "I feel..."

- Acknowledge that your feelings are valid and deserve to be heard and respected.

Need:
- Reflect on the underlying needs or values that are driving your feelings.

- Consider what fundamental human needs are not being met or are being threatened in the situation.

- Be specific about the needs that are important to you and why they matter.

- Focus on universal human needs such as safety, respect, understanding, connection, autonomy, and fairness.

Request (or Action):
- Clearly communicate a specific request or action that would help meet your needs and address the situation constructively.

- Make your request actionable, feasible, and respectful.

- Be open to negotiation and compromise, allowing the other person to respond with their perspective and needs.

- Avoid making demands or ultimatums. Instead, frame your request as a sincere invitation for collaboration and mutual understanding.

By following these steps, you can effectively apply the NVC model to communicate with empathy, authenticity, and clarity, fostering deeper connections, understanding, and harmony in your relationships.

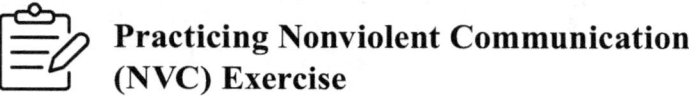

Practicing Nonviolent Communication (NVC) Exercise

Take a moment to guide yourself through the steps of nonviolent communication outlined below. Pause to reflect on each step as you progress.

Observation: Start by observing a recent situation in your relationship that caused tension or conflict. Describe the situation objectively, focusing on facts rather than interpretations or judgments. For example, "During dinner last night, when I expressed my concerns about your drinking, you raised your voice and became defensive."

Feelings: Identify and express your feelings about the situation. Use "I" statements to take ownership of your emotions. For instance, "I felt frustrated and hurt when you raised your voice because I want us to communicate calmly and respectfully."

Needs: Reflect on the underlying needs or values that were not met in the situation. Consider what you were seeking or hoping for in that moment. For example, "I need to feel heard and understood in our conversations about your drinking because I value open communication and mutual respect in our relationship."

Request or Action: Formulate a specific request or action that would address your unmet needs and improve the situation. Be clear and concise in expressing what you would like to see happen. For instance, "I would appreciate it if we could set aside time to discuss our concerns about your drinking without interruptions, and agree on a plan together to address it."

Role-Playing Practice Exercise: Practice applying the NVC model in a role-playing scenario with a friend or quietly to yourself. Take turns portraying different roles and engaging in a dialogue using the four steps of observation, feelings, needs, and requests. Use this opportunity to refine and proactice your communication skills and deepen your understanding in a safe environment. At first it takes time to walk through these steps.

Reflection: After completing the exercise, take some time to reflect on your experience. Notice any insights or shifts in your communication style and how it felt to express yourself using the NVC model. Consider how you can incorporate these principles into your everyday interactions to foster healthier and more harmonious relationships.

By practicing Nonviolent Communication (NVC) regularly, you can cultivate greater empathy, understanding, and connection in your relationships, leading to more effective conflict resolution and mutual respect.

In tandem with setting boundaries, NVC serves as a powerful tool for navigating difficult conversations and making informed decisions about our relationships. By expressing ourselves authentically and listening compassionately to ourselves, we cultivate deeper awareness and foster environments where growth and transformation are possible. Effective communication, grounded in principles of empathy and self-awareness, is vital for navigating boundaries in relationships. Nonviolent Communication (NVC) offers a valuable toolkit for expressing needs, establishing boundaries, and fostering understanding, particularly in relationships affected by addiction. Continued practice of NVC principles can lead to healthier communication patterns and more fulfilling relationships.

To Summarize

Navigating relationships affected by addiction presents numerous challenges, but understanding and implementing boundaries effectively can empower individuals to prioritize their well-being and navigate these complexities with confidence. By recognizing boundaries as acts of self-care and knowing their limits, individuals can assert their needs, values, and expectations within relationships, fostering understanding, respect, and mutual support. Establishing personal boundaries and knowing when to assert them are crucial components of maintaining emotional balance, preserving self-respect, and nurturing healthy connections amidst the challenges of addiction. Ultimately, by embracing boundaries as affirmations of self-care and empowerment, individuals can navigate relationships impacted by addiction with resilience, compassion, and integrity.

In relationships impacted by addiction, empowered decision-making and effective communication are essential pillars for navigating challenges and fostering healthier dynamics. Understanding one's limits and utilizing tools like Nonviolent Communication (NVC) offer invaluable insights and strategies for asserting boundaries, advocating for one's needs, and making informed choices. By embracing self-awareness, clarity, and empathy, individuals can cultivate environments where mutual respect and understanding thrive, paving the way for deeper connections and greater well-being.

Key Insights

Establishing Personal Boundaries as Acts of Self-Care: One key insight from navigating relationships affected by addiction is the importance of establishing personal boundaries as acts of self-care. Boundaries serve as guidelines for prioritizing our mental health and well-being, providing a framework for asserting our needs and values within relationships. By setting clear boundaries, we affirm our self-worth and empower ourselves to create environments that support our emotional and psychological health. Recognizing boundaries as affirmations of self-care shifts the focus from attempting to control others' behavior to prioritizing our own needs and values.

Knowing Your Limits Empowers Effective Boundary Setting: Another crucial insight is the empowering nature of knowing your limits in effective boundary setting. Understanding your limits involves self-awareness, introspection, and recognizing when certain behaviors or situations compromise your emotional well-being. By knowing your limits, you gain the confidence to establish and maintain healthy boundaries in your relationships, communicating your needs and expectations assertively. This awareness fosters self-respect, empowers decision-making aligned with your values, and contributes to the cultivation of healthy and fulfilling relationships.

Clarity and Empowerment Through Boundary-setting: Recognizing and honoring personal limits enables individuals to gain clarity about their needs and priorities in relationships affected by addiction. This clarity empowers individuals to assert boundaries confidently, advocate for themselves, and make decisions aligned with their well-being.

Enhanced Communication with Nonviolent Communication (NVC): NVC offers a framework for clearer communication, self-awareness, and conflict resolution, particularly in emotionally charged situations. By prioritizing empathy, clarity, and nonjudgmental communication, individuals can navigate boundaries assertively and foster healthier relationships, even amidst the complexities of addiction.

Consolidating Our Insights: Understanding the importance of boundaries and limits in our relationships is essential for navigating tough relationship decisions. By recognizing when someone has crossed the line and protecting our well-being, we empower ourselves to make informed choices about whether to stay or go. Learning to navigate boundaries informs our decisions by helping us understand our needs and values more clearly.

Making empowered decisions based on limits enables us to prioritize our well-being and happiness, even in challenging situations. By communicating and navigating boundaries with non-violent communication, we create a foundation of trust and understanding in our relationships. This approach fosters healthy communication and mutual respect, which are vital for making tough decisions.

Overall, these insights support our enlightenment and self-discovery journey by empowering us with self-awareness and clarity. As we navigate tough relationship decisions touched by addiction, we are guided by the love and support of those around us, creating a safe and nurturing environment for growth and healing.

Reflection: *Reflecting on the importance of boundaries and limits in relationships, consider the following: How has recognizing and enforcing boundaries empowered you? In what ways have you protected your well-being by setting and maintaining boundaries? How can non-violent communication techniques help foster healthy communication and personal well-being in your relationships? Think about how these insights have contributed to your self-awareness and clarity as you navigate a relationship touched by addiction.*

CHAPTER 6

WITH OR WITHOUT YOU

Exploring Your Options: Finding Your Path Forward

Introduction

In this chapter, we go on a journey of self-discovery and empowerment as we navigate the complexities of relationships affected by addiction. The decision to stay, leave, or find a middle ground is deeply personal and laden with emotional weight, requiring careful consideration and introspection. As we delve into this pivotal decision-making process, we will explore alternative approaches beyond the conventional options, recognizing the multifaceted nature of our circumstances. We'll begin by weighing the pros and cons of each option, contemplating both short-term repercussions and long-term implications.

Additionally, we'll delve into the psychology model of change, offering valuable insights into our readiness for transformation and the dynamics of our relationship with our addicted loved one. Along the way, we'll confront the fears that may be holding us back, acknowledging their influence on our decision-making process and envisioning a future where fear no longer dictates our choices. Join us as we embark on a journey of self-discovery, empowerment, and resilience, seeking our path forward with clarity and purpose.

Navigating the Decision: Stay, Leave, or Find a Middle Ground

The decision to stay in a relationship, leave, or find a middle ground is one of the most significant and deeply personal choices one can make. It requires careful consideration, self-reflection, and an honest evaluation of the situation at hand. In this section, we'll explore how to navigate this decision-making process with thoughtfulness and clarity.

Weighing the Pros and Cons:

Before making a decision, it's essential to weigh the pros and cons of each option. Consider both the short-term and long-term implications of continuing the relationship. Reflect on what aspects of the relationship bring you joy and fulfillment, and what challenges or issues you are facing. Conducting a thought experiment can help clarify your thoughts:

Thought Experiment: Staying

Imagine the relationship improving over time. What positive changes would need to occur for you to feel satisfied and fulfilled? Conversely, consider what would happen if the situation worsened. What steps could you take to protect your well-being and maintain your boundaries?

Thought Experiment: Leaving

Envision life without the relationship. What opportunities for growth and self-discovery might arise? Acknowledge the challenges of starting anew, but also consider the potential for personal growth and fulfillment.

No one can make this decision for you.

Powerful Questions to Ask Yourself

Here are five powerful questions to reflect on to help you discover where you stand:

- What are my core values and priorities in a relationship?

- How do I feel when I imagine staying in the relationship? How about leaving?

- What support systems do I have in place to help me navigate this decision?

- Am I willing to put in the effort and work required to improve the relationship, if that's the path I choose?

- What fears or concerns are holding me back from making a decision?

By reflecting on these questions and exploring the thought experiments, you can gain a deeper understanding of your feelings and motivations. Remember, the decision to stay, leave, or find a middle ground is yours to make, and it's okay to take the time you need to arrive at the right choice for you. And even when you think you've made a decision, it's important to recognize that feelings and circumstances can change. Be kind to yourself and offer yourself compassion throughout this process.

Navigating the decision to stay or leave a relationship affected by addiction involves grappling with various complex factors. First, there's the long-term investment of time, energy, and emotions, which can create a strong attachment that makes it hard to let go. Family considerations add another layer of complexity, particularly if there are children involved, as the decision can profoundly impact their well-being and future. Financial entanglements, such as shared assets and financial dependence, further complicate matters, as does the pressure of societal and cultural expectations, which may influence one's decision to maintain the status quo. Fear of the unknown, including uncertainty about the future and the prospect of being alone, can also fuel hesitation and indecision. Emotional attachment to the partner, despite the challenges faced, can make envisioning a life without them daunting. Additionally, feelings of guilt or obligation towards loved ones, as well as the hope that the relationship can improve, contribute to a sense of ambivalence and uncertainty.

The Power of Change and Motivation for Change:

Understanding the Psychology Model of Change for Yourself

The psychology model of change, often referred to as the Transtheoretical Model of Change (TTM), outlines the stages individuals go through when making significant life changes. These stages include precontemplation, contemplation, preparation, action, maintenance, and termination. Reflecting on where you currently stand in this model can provide insight into your readiness and willingness to make changes in your life, including decisions regarding your relationship with your addicted loved one. Let's dig into this deeper.

Let's elaborate on each stage of the Transtheoretical Model of Change (TTM) and relate them to the staying and leaving process in the context of a loved one of an addict:

Precontemplation:

Precontemplation is the stage where individuals are not yet considering changing their behavior. They may be unaware of the need for change, in denial about the consequences of their actions, or resistant to acknowledging the problem. In the context of a loved one of an addict, this stage might manifest as being unaware or denying the severity of the addiction's impact on their relationship. They may be reluctant to acknowledge the need for change or may feel overwhelmed by the prospect of addressing the issue.

Contemplation:

Contemplation is the stage where individuals begin to recognize the need for change but may still feel ambivalent about taking action. They may weigh the pros and cons of changing their behavior and may experience feelings of uncertainty or indecision. In the context of a loved one of an addict, this stage might involve recognizing the negative effects of the addiction on their relationship and considering the possibility of making changes. They may feel torn between the desire to stay and the fear of leaving.

Preparation:

Preparation is the stage where individuals are actively preparing to make a change. They may begin gathering information, seeking support, or making plans to address the problem. In the context of a loved one of an addict, this stage might involve researching treatment options, attending support groups, or seeking counseling for themselves. They may start to set boundaries or explore the possibility of intervention or professional help for their loved one.

Action:

Action is the stage where individuals take concrete steps towards changing their behavior. They may implement new strategies, adopt healthier habits, or seek professional assistance to address the problem. In the context of a loved one of an addict, this stage might involve implementing boundaries, seeking therapy or support groups, or encouraging their loved one to enter treatment. They may actively work towards improving their relationship dynamics and addressing the impact of addiction on their lives.

Maintenance:

Maintenance is the stage where individuals work to sustain the changes they have made over the long term. They may develop coping strategies, seek ongoing support, and actively prevent relapse into old patterns of behavior. In the context of a loved one of an addict, this stage might involve continuing to enforce boundaries, attending therapy or support groups, and prioritizing self-care. They may navigate challenges and setbacks while remaining committed to their own well-being and the health of their relationship.

Termination:

Termination is the final stage where individuals have successfully integrated the changes into their lives, and the problem behavior is no longer a significant concern. They may feel confident in their ability to maintain the changes and may no longer experience temptation or urges related to the problem behavior. In the context of a loved one of an addict, this stage might involve reaching a point where the relationship is no longer negatively impacted by the addiction. They may have established healthy boundaries, addressed underlying issues, and found a sense of peace and fulfillment in their lives.

By understanding the stages of change outlined in the Transtheoretical Model (TTM), we gain valuable insight into our own journey of transformation. Whether we're contemplating staying or leaving a relationship affected by addiction, the model provides a roadmap for self-reflection and growth. By recognizing where we are in the process, we can better understand our motivations, fears, and aspirations. This awareness empowers us to make informed decisions, take proactive steps towards change, and prioritize our well-being. Remember, change is a gradual and nonlinear process, and it's okay to move through the stages at your own pace. Trust in your ability to navigate the complexities of your situation and know that you're not alone on this journey. Each step forward, no matter how small, brings you closer to a healthier and happier future.

Motivation for Change in Relation to the Addicted Loved One in Your Life

Just as you can explore your own motivation for change, it's essential to consider the motivation for change in your addicted loved one. Addiction often involves cycles of denial, ambivalence, and resistance to change. Understanding where your loved one may be on the spectrum of readiness for change can help you manage your expectations and tailor your approach accordingly. How can this model help you in decision making? By recognizing where you and your loved one are on the psychology model of change, you gain valuable insights that can inform your decision-making process. For example, if you are in the contemplation stage while your loved one is in precontemplation, it may be unrealistic to expect immediate change. Understanding these dynamics can help you set realistic goals and boundaries, while also fostering empathy and compassion for both yourself and your loved one.

Recognizing Intrinsic Motivation for Change involves understanding the concept of intrinsic motivation and acknowledging that we cannot make someone else change. Intrinsic motivation refers to the internal drive that comes from within oneself, rooted in personal values, goals, and aspirations. It is the genuine desire for growth and improvement, driven by an individual's own sense of purpose and fulfillment. Importantly, intrinsic motivation cannot be imposed or forced upon another person. Each individual must find their own motivation for change, and we cannot control or dictate this process for others. Whether we decide to stay in the relationship or leave, it's crucial to focus on our own intrinsic motivation for change. By connecting with our inner values and aspirations, we can empower ourselves to make decisions that prioritize our well-being and lead us towards a healthier and happier future. Ultimately, we can only control our own actions and choices, and recognizing our intrinsic motivation allows us to take ownership of our lives and navigate the challenges of relationships affected by addiction with clarity and resilience.

Navigating the Waiting Game

Many individuals find themselves waiting for their addicted loved one to seek recovery, holding onto hope for positive change. While this hope is understandable and often rooted in genuine concern and love, it's crucial to recognize that change may not happen on your timeline. Instead of passively waiting, focus on taking proactive steps to support your own well-being and seek resources and guidance to navigate the complexities of addiction.

Recognizing intrinsic motivation for change involves understanding the concept of intrinsic motivation and acknowledging that we cannot make someone else change. Intrinsic motivation refers to the internal drive that comes from within oneself, rooted in personal values, goals, and aspirations. It is the genuine desire for growth and improvement, driven by an individual's own sense of purpose and fulfillment. Importantly, intrinsic motivation cannot be imposed or forced upon another person. Each individual must find their own motivation for change, and we cannot control or dictate this process for others. Whether we decide to stay in the relationship or leave, it's crucial to focus on our own intrinsic motivation for change. By connecting with our inner values and aspirations, we can empower ourselves to make decisions that prioritize our well-being and lead us towards a healthier and happier future. Ultimately, we can only control our own actions and choices, and recognizing our intrinsic motivation allows us to take ownership of our lives and navigate the challenges of relationships affected by addiction with clarity and resilience.

The goal of this exploration is to help you gain awareness and feel empowered to safeguard your well-being, regardless of the decisions you make. By recognizing that there is no right or wrong answer, you free yourself from the burden of external expectations and judgments. Embrace the fluidity of decision-making, knowing that it's okay to change your mind and adjust your path as needed. Ultimately, the psychology of change invites you to embrace the journey of self-discovery and transformation. Whether you decide to stay in the relationship, leave, or find a middle ground, know that your choices are valid and deserving of respect. By honoring your own needs and priorities, you pave the way for a future filled with growth, resilience, and well-being.

A Note on Transition: Transitioning in Relationships Touched by Addiction

It's crucial to recognize that navigating a relationship impacted by addiction often involves periods of transition. In these phases, we find ourselves grappling with complex emotions and uncertainties, unsure of whether to stay or go. Transition is a state of flux, a phase where we may not have all the answers, where clarity eludes us, and where decisions may feel daunting.

Transition, in essence, signifies a journey—a movement from one state to another. It's a process of evolving, of moving through uncertainty towards clarity. While in transition, we may find ourselves in a state of limbo, unsure of what the future holds or which direction to take. And yet, it's precisely within this state of transition that self-compassion becomes paramount.

Transition offers us the opportunity to extend kindness and understanding to ourselves as we navigate the complexities of our emotions and decisions. It's a reminder that it's okay not to have all the answers, that uncertainty is a natural part of the human experience. By embracing the perspective of transition, we grant ourselves the grace to explore, to gather information, and to allow ourselves the time and space needed to reach a place of clarity.

Transition invites us to adopt a more positive outlook on the journey ahead. Rather than viewing our indecision as a source of frustration or inadequacy, we can recognize it as a natural part of the process—a necessary step towards finding resolution. It acknowledges that we are in a state of growth, of learning, and of discovery.

Moreover, the perspective of transition fosters compassion towards ourselves as we grapple with tough decisions. It reminds us that it's okay to feel uncertain, to waver in our convictions, and to take our time in reaching conclusions. Transition offers us the freedom to explore different possibilities, to gather insights, and to ultimately make decisions that align with our values and well-being.

So, if you find yourself in a stage of transition in your relationship affected by addiction, remember to be gentle with yourself. Allow yourself the space to navigate the uncertainties with patience and self-compassion. Embrace the journey of transition as an opportunity for growth, learning, and self-discovery. And above all, trust that clarity will come in its own time, guiding you toward decisions that honor your truth and well-being.

Acknowledging Fear: Nurturing Compassion Amidst Uncertainty

Fear is a powerful emotion that can profoundly influence our thoughts, feelings, and actions, particularly in the context of relationships affected by addiction. It manifests in various forms, such as fear of change, uncertainty about the future, or guilt over potential outcomes. These fears often serve as barriers that hold us back from making decisions aligned with our well-being and values.

Identifying Potential Fears: In examining your situation, it's important to consider the possible fears that may be influencing your decision-making process. Are you afraid of change, of stepping into the unknown? Do feelings of uncertainty about the future leave you feeling paralyzed? Are you grappling with guilt, whether it's guilt over potentially abandoning your partner or guilt over prioritizing your own needs?

Fear Keeping You in the Relationship: One of the fears that may be keeping you in the relationship is the fear of being alone or starting over. You may fear losing the comfort and familiarity of your current situation, even if it's not ideal. Additionally, fear of judgment from others or societal expectations about relationships may contribute to your hesitation to leave.

Fear Driving You to Leave: Conversely, fear may also be driving your desire to leave the relationship. You may fear the consequences of staying in a situation that compromises your well-being or the well-being of your loved ones. Fear of continued pain, disappointment, or harm may motivate you to seek a path of separation.

Role of Fear in Decision-Making: Fear often plays a significant role in decision-making, clouding our judgment and influencing our perceptions of risk and reward. It can lead us to prioritize short-term comfort over long-term happiness or compel us to avoid taking necessary steps toward growth and change.

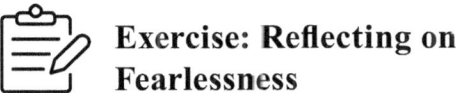

Exercise: Reflecting on Fearlessness

Take a moment to envision a scenario where fear plays no role in your decision-making process regarding your relationship. If you were completely free from fear, what action would you take? How might your decision differ from your current situation? This exercise can offer valuable insight into your true desires and values, allowing you to explore possibilities with a clear and fearless perspective.

In To Summarize, acknowledging and confronting fear is essential in navigating relationships affected by addiction. By identifying and understanding the fears that influence our decisions, we can gain clarity and empowerment to make choices that prioritize our well-being and happiness, ultimately leading to a path of growth and fulfillment.

Staying vs. Leaving: Exploring Other Options

While staying in the relationship or leaving may seem like the only two options, it's essential to recognize that there may be other paths forward. Let's explore the concept of change and some alternative approaches to navigating relationships affected by addiction.

Taking Time Away: Sometimes, stepping back from the relationship temporarily can provide clarity and perspective. Taking a break allows both parties to reflect on their needs and priorities without the pressure of immediate decisions.

Implementing a Safe-for-Now Approach: This approach involves establishing temporary boundaries or agreements to create a safer and healthier environment within the relationship. It may involve setting specific conditions for continued engagement, such as seeking professional help or attending therapy together.

Love from a Distance: In some cases, maintaining a physical distance from your loved one may be necessary to protect your well-being. This approach allows you to focus on your own healing and growth while still offering support from afar.

Focus on You: Taking time to prioritize self-care and personal development can be a powerful alternative to staying or leaving. Investing in your own well-being and happiness can lead to greater resilience and empowerment, regardless of the status of your relationship.

Seek Professional Support: Consulting with a therapist, counselor, or support group specializing in addiction can provide invaluable guidance and perspective. Professional support can help you navigate complex emotions, set healthy boundaries, and explore potential solutions tailored to your unique situation.

Couples Therapy: Engaging in couples therapy with a qualified therapist experienced in addiction can offer a structured and supportive environment for addressing relationship challenges. Couples therapy can facilitate open communication, improve conflict resolution skills, and foster mutual understanding and empathy.

Establish Boundaries with Flexibility: Instead of rigidly adhering to binary options of staying or leaving, consider establishing boundaries with flexibility. This approach allows for fluid adjustments based on changing circumstances and individual needs. It may involve setting clear boundaries while remaining open to reassessing and renegotiating them over time.

Practice Harm Reduction: If leaving the relationship is not immediately feasible or desirable, consider implementing harm reduction strategies to minimize the negative impact of addiction on your life. This approach focuses on reducing the harmful consequences of substance use while acknowledging the complexities of addiction.

Focus on Personal Growth: Use this challenging period as an opportunity for personal growth and self-discovery. Invest time and energy in activities that nourish your mind, body, and spirit, such as hobbies, self-care practices, or pursuing educational or career goals. Cultivating resilience and self-awareness can empower you to navigate challenges with greater strength and clarity.

Explore Collaborative Solutions: Engage in open and honest communication with your addicted loved one to explore collaborative solutions aimed at mutual well-being. This may involve brainstorming creative ways to address challenges, seeking alternative forms of support, or jointly committing to positive changes and recovery efforts.

Seeking Support: You're Not Alone. Utilizing resources and support networks to explore options and receive guidance from others who understand your situation. Engaging with support networks, such as friends, family members, support groups, (S.Y.K.M. FaceBook Support Group) or online communities, can provide invaluable emotional support, validation, and practical advice. Connecting with others who have experienced similar challenges can offer a sense of connection and empowerment, reminding you that you're not alone on this journey. By reaching out for support, you can gain new perspectives, access helpful resources, and find strength in community as you navigate the complexities of relationships affected by addiction.

Remember, there are always ways to navigate this tough situation, and you will ultimately do what feels right for you. It's okay if your feelings and decisions shift and change over time. The most important thing is to honor yourself and prioritize your own well-being as you navigate this journey.

To Summarize

In navigating the complexities of relationships affected by addiction, we've went on a journey of self-discovery and empowerment, seeking our path forward with clarity and purpose. Throughout this chapter, we've grappled with the deeply personal decision of whether to stay, leave, or find a middle ground, recognizing the weight of each option and the emotional complexities involved. We've explored alternative approaches beyond the conventional dichotomy, acknowledging the multifaceted nature of our circumstances and the myriad paths available to us. By weighing the pros and cons of each option, contemplating the psychology model of change, and confronting our fears head-on, we've gained valuable insights into our readiness for transformation and the dynamics of our relationships. As we envision a future where fear no longer dictates our choices, we embrace the notion of agency and empowerment, recognizing that our well-being is ultimately in our own hands. Though the path forward may be fraught with challenges and uncertainties, we move forward with resilience and determination, empowered to forge our own path towards a healthier and happier future, with or without our addicted loved one.

Key Insights

Navigating the Decision: Stay, Leave, or Find a Middle Ground: Recognize the deeply personal nature of the decision and explore alternative approaches beyond the traditional options.

Weighing the Pros and Cons: Reflect on the short-term and long-term implications of each option and conduct thought experiments to clarify your thoughts.

Understanding the Psychology Model of Change: Gain insight into your readiness for change and the dynamics of your relationship with your addicted loved one by exploring the stages of change outlined in the Transtheoretical Model.

Acknowledging Fear: Identify and address the fears that may be holding you back from making a decision aligned with your well-being, and envision a scenario where fear plays no role in your decision-making process.

Consolidating Our Insights: Exploring our options is crucial when deciding whether to stay or go in a relationship affected by addiction. Understanding the stages of change in relation to our addicted loved one provides clarity and insight into the dynamics at play. By considering different options for moving forward, we gain a sense of agency and empowerment in our decision-making process.

Identifying potential fears surrounding our choices can help us address and overcome them, allowing us to make decisions from a place of strength and courage. This exploration of options and fears is instrumental in our enlightenment and self-discovery journey, as it empowers us with self-awareness and clarity.

Ultimately, this process supports us in navigating tough relationship decisions touched by addiction. With a deeper understanding of our options and fears, we can move forward with confidence, knowing that we are making choices that align with our values and well-being.

> **Reflection:** *Reflecting on the importance of exploring options in tough relationship decisions, consider the following: How has exploring different options empowered you in your decision-making process? Have you encountered any fears or obstacles in considering your choices, and how have you addressed them? In what ways has this exploration of options contributed to your self-awareness and clarity? Think about how understanding the stages of change in relation to your addicted loved one has influenced your perspective on the situation.*

CHAPTER 7

IF YOU COULD READ MY MIND

Trusting Your Instincts: Finding Clarity

Introduction

Welcome to the compassionate exploration of "If You Could Read My Mind," where we delve into the intricacies of navigating relationships touched by addiction. This chapter invites us to journey inward, to connect deeply with our inner voice, cultivate self-awareness, and embrace self-compassion as we navigate the complexities of tough relationship decisions.

In the midst of uncertainty and emotional turmoil, our inner voice serves as a guiding light, offering insights and wisdom beyond the realm of logic. Through introspection and mindfulness practices, we uncover the depths of our desires and aspirations, gaining clarity about what truly matters to us.

Central to our journey is the recognition of the importance of our values—the guiding principles that anchor us in authenticity and integrity. Reflecting on our values empowers us to make decisions aligned with our true selves, fostering deeper connections and greater fulfillment in our relationships.

As we navigate the emotional storms of relationships affected by addiction, self-compassion becomes our refuge—a source of solace and strength in challenging times. By honoring our feelings and nurturing our inner voice, we cultivate resilience and understanding, fostering deeper connection and compassion in our relationships.

The phrase "if you could read my mind" reflects the inner turmoil and complexity of emotions that one experiences, especially when navigating relationships affected by addiction. It's a sentiment that captures the whirlwind of thoughts, feelings, and urges that often consume our minds in such situations.

In the context of this chapter, "if you could read my mind" symbolizes the unspoken struggles and challenges that we grapple with internally. It's a recognition of the profound disconnect between our inner experiences and the external reality of our relationships. Despite our silent cries for understanding and empathy, our addicted loved ones may remain oblivious to the depth of our emotional turmoil due to the selfish nature of addiction.

This chapter emphasizes the importance of acknowledging and honoring our internal experiences. It highlights the significance of getting quiet, listening to our intuition, and tuning into our inner voice amidst the chaos of addiction. By doing so, we empower ourselves to navigate the complexities of relationships with clarity, authenticity, and resilience.

Self-Reflection: Listen to Your Inner Voice and Intuition

Have you ever stopped to reflect on the intricate nature of your thoughts, envisioning how someone, particularly your addicted loved one, might react if they could perceive your innermost thoughts, especially those guiding your decision to stay or leave?

Engaging in introspection and self-reflection is a cornerstone of positive psychology, offering individuals a pathway to gain clarity, insight, and authenticity in their lives, particularly in the realm of relationships. By delving into their inner world through practices like journaling, meditation, or guided reflection exercises, individuals can tap into the wisdom of their thoughts, feelings, and intuition, guiding their decision-making process and aligning their actions with their values and goals.

Understanding Intuition

Intuition, often described as a gut feeling or instinct, is a powerful form of inner guidance that transcends logical reasoning. It arises from the subconscious mind and can provide valuable insights into situations, relationships, and decisions. By paying attention to subtle cues, sensations, and hunches, individuals can harness the wisdom of their intuition to navigate complex situations and make choices that resonate with their innermost desires and values.

Trusting Your Inner Voice

Your inner voice is the essence of your true self, speaking to you through thoughts, feelings, and intuitive nudges. Trusting your inner voice involves cultivating self-awareness, discernment, and self-trust. It requires quieting the noise of external influences and tuning into the whispers of your heart and soul. By honoring your inner voice and listening to its guidance, you can make decisions that are authentic, aligned, and empowering.

The Power of Introspection

Introspection involves diving deep into your inner world to explore your thoughts, emotions, and beliefs. It allows you to gain clarity about your values, strengths, and aspirations, as well as understand how past experiences may be shaping your present reality. Through introspection, you can uncover hidden patterns, identify areas for growth, and cultivate self-awareness and self-compassion. By regularly engaging in introspective practices, such as journaling, meditation, or contemplative reflection, you can deepen your understanding of yourself and your relationships, paving the way for greater clarity, authenticity, and fulfillment.

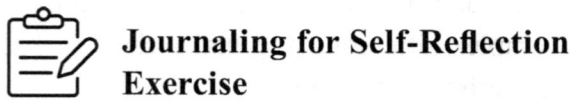
Journaling for Self-Reflection Exercise

Journaling is a powerful tool for introspection and self-reflection, allowing you to explore your thoughts, emotions, and beliefs in a structured and therapeutic manner. Here's a simple journaling exercise to deepen your understanding of yourself and your relationships:

Set aside dedicated time:
Find a quiet and comfortable space where you can journal without distractions. Set aside a specific time each day or week for your journaling practice.

Reflect on your experiences:
Begin by reflecting on recent experiences in your life, particularly those related to your relationships. Consider moments of joy, challenges, conflicts, or growth opportunities.

Explore your thoughts and emotions:
Write freely about your thoughts, feelings, and reactions to these experiences. Allow yourself to express whatever comes to mind without judgment or censorship. Use prompts such as:

- What emotions am I experiencing in this situation?
- What thoughts or beliefs are influencing my perceptions?
- How do these experiences align with my values and aspirations?

Identify patterns and themes:
As you journal, look for recurring patterns, themes, or insights that emerge from your reflections. Pay attention to any insights about your values, strengths, or areas for growth.

Cultivate self-awareness and self-compassion: Practice self-compassion as you explore your inner world. Be gentle and nonjudgmental with yourself, acknowledging that introspection is a journey of self-discovery and growth.

Set intentions for growth:
Based on your reflections, identify specific areas for personal or relational growth. Set intentions or goals for how you'd like to cultivate greater clarity, authenticity, or fulfillment in your relationships.

Review and revisit:
Regularly review your journal entries to track your progress and insights over time. Revisit past entries to gain new perspectives or insights into your experiences and relationships.

By regularly engaging in journaling for self-reflection, you can deepen your understanding of yourself and your relationships, uncover hidden patterns, and cultivate greater self-awareness and self-compassion. This practice can pave the way for greater clarity, authenticity, and fulfillment in your life.

Cultivating Mindfulness and Self-Reflection

Mindfulness practices promote present-moment awareness and non-judgmental acceptance of one's thoughts, feelings, and experiences. In relationships, mindfulness can help individuals tune into their emotions, needs, and the dynamics of their interactions with others. By cultivating mindfulness through meditation, mindful listening, or body scans, individuals can gain clarity about the direction they want their relationships to take. Additionally, self-reflection exercises, such as journaling or contemplative practices, can provide insights into relationship patterns, preferences, and areas for growth, fostering greater clarity and intentionality in navigating relationships.

In essence, listening to your inner voice, trusting your intuition, and engaging in introspection and self-reflection are essential tools for navigating relationships with clarity, authenticity, and wisdom. By honoring the wisdom of your inner world, you can cultivate deeper connections, make empowered decisions, and lead a life that aligns with your true essence and purpose.

Overcoming Inner Obstacles: Empowering Your Mind Through Cognitive Challenges

Have you ever found yourself trapped in the grip of feelings of depression or anxiety when loving an addict? It can feel as though the brightness of life is just out of reach, leaving you stuck in a dark, suffocating haze with seemingly no escape. But fear not – there is hope. Cognitive Behavioral Therapy (CBT) offers a beacon of light in these dark moments, providing techniques to challenge the potential negative thoughts and behaviors that keep us stuck in despair.

At its core, CBT explores the stories we tell ourselves and their profound impact on our thoughts, emotions, and actions. Through the ABC model – where A represents external events, B symbolizes beliefs, and C signifies resulting consequences – we uncover the intricate interplay between our interpretations of events and our subsequent behaviors. This process shines a light on the negative cycles of thinking that could ensnare us, fostering a tendency to depression, anxiety, stress, and a host of other detrimental behaviors.

Yet, there is hope on the horizon. By identifying and challenging these patterns, CBT can be a powerful tool in breaking free from the holds of negativity. This process, known as cognitive restructuring, involves three pivotal steps: recognizing unhelpful thoughts, evaluating evidence both for and against these thoughts, and ultimately formulating a rational, constructive alternative.

Imagine, for instance, an addicted loved one avoids coming home and leaves you feeling unlovable, unsexy and destined for a lifetime of solitude. Through cognitive restructuring, you begin to question the validity of this belief, uncovering evidence to the contrary – evidence that reminds you of your worth and capacity for connection.

But perhaps one of the most transformative aspects of CBT lies in its concept of taking our thinking to court. This metaphorical courtroom offers a space for us to interrogate our thoughts, challenging their validity and exploring alternative perspectives. By repeatedly asking ourselves, "Is this true?" and providing evidence to the contrary, we gradually chip away at the foundations of our self-defeating beliefs.

And yet, cognitive restructuring is just one facet of the broader landscape of mindfulness-based cognitive therapy (MBCT). Unlike CBT, which focuses on challenging and restructuring unwanted thoughts, MBCT encourages us to embrace the present moment – to be, rather than to do. Through mindfulness exercises like walking meditation, we learn to anchor ourselves in the here and now, releasing the grip of past regrets and future anxieties.

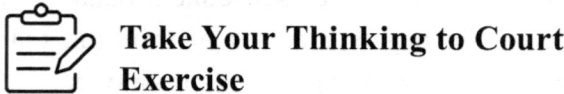 **Take Your Thinking to Court Exercise**

Step 1: Identify the Negative Thought
Start by identifying a negative thought you've been having about yourself. It could be something like "I'm not good enough" or "I'll never succeed."

Step 2: Question the Validity
Write down the negative thought and ask yourself, "Is this true?" Then, fill in the blank: "That's not true because..."

Step 3: Provide Evidence
List at least three pieces of evidence to refute the negative thought. For example:

- "I've succeeded in the past."
- "People have complimented me on my work."
- "I have valuable skills and talents."

Step 4: Repeat the Question
After providing evidence, ask yourself again, "Is this true?" Then, fill in the blank: "Another way to see this is..."

Step 5: Evaluate Harmfulness
Finally, ask yourself, "Is this thought helpful or harmful?" Reflect on how the thought impacts your emotions and behaviors. If it's harmful, challenge it further using the techniques above.

Step 6: Explore Alternative Perspectives
Come up with at least three alternative perspectives or interpretations of the situation. For instance:

- "I may face setbacks, but they don't define my worth."
- "I'm a work in progress, and it's okay to make mistakes."
- "Challenges help me grow and learn."

Remember, the goal of this exercise is to challenge negative self-talk, explore alternative perspectives, and cultivate self-compassion. By taking your thinking to court in this way, you can begin to shift towards more positive and empowering beliefs about yourself.

In essence, whether through the structured strategies of CBT or the contemplative practices of MBCT, the journey toward overcoming depression and anxiety is one of self-compassion and empowerment. So as you navigate your inner landscape, remember to extend yourself the kindness and understanding you so readily offer to others. After all, in the face of life's challenges, a little self-compassion can go a long way.

Navigating Emotional Turmoil: Embracing the Storm

Have you ever found yourself tiptoeing through an emotional minefield in a relationship impacted by addiction, hesitant to express your true feelings for fear of igniting conflict or worsening the situation?

The Dangers of Bottling Up Emotions

Bottling up emotions is a common phenomenon in which individuals suppress or repress their feelings instead of expressing them openly. This may occur for various reasons, including fear of judgment or rejection, societal expectations, or a desire to maintain a façade of strength and composure. However, while bottling up emotions may provide temporary relief, it is not a healthy long-term coping strategy.

When we bottle up our emotions, we prevent ourselves from processing and releasing them in a healthy manner. This can lead to a buildup of emotional pressure, akin to a pressure cooker, where the intensity of our feelings continues to escalate over time. Eventually, the pressure becomes too much to contain, resulting in an emotional outburst or breakdown. Additionally, bottling up emotions can cause us to become disconnected from ourselves and others, leading to feelings of isolation and loneliness.

Emotional Intelligence: The Power of Emotions as Communicators

Emotions serve as powerful communicators, providing valuable insight into our inner world and guiding our actions. When we experience anger, it's often a signal that our boundaries have been crossed or that something is unjust. Similarly, feelings of fear alert us to potential threats or dangers, prompting us to take necessary precautions. On the other hand, joy serves as an indicator that we are aligned with our desires and moving towards experiences that bring us fulfillment. By acknowledging and honoring our emotions, we gain a deeper understanding of ourselves and our needs, allowing us to navigate life with greater clarity and authenticity. Embrace your emotions as messengers, guiding you towards alignment and authenticity in your journey of self-discovery and growth.

Reflective Question: *How can acknowledging and understanding the messages conveyed by our emotions enhance our ability to navigate life's challenges with greater clarity and purpose?*

Moreover, suppressing emotions can have detrimental effects on our mental and physical health. Research has shown that chronic emotional suppression is associated with increased stress levels, anxiety, depression, and even physical health problems such as hypertension and weakened immune function. By denying ourselves the opportunity to acknowledge and process our emotions, we deprive ourselves of the chance to find resolution and healing.

Navigating the Minefield: Understanding Why We Bottle Up Emotions in Relationships Affected by Addiction

Having tough conversations is never easy. Whether it's addressing how someone's actions are hurting you or confronting a loved one struggling with addiction, the prospect of these discussions can be daunting. The tough conversations and my desire to figure things out are some of the major reasons I often thought to myself if you could only read my mind.

Firstly, it's essential to acknowledge why these conversations are difficult. They often evoke a primal fear of confrontation, stemming from our inherent desire to avoid conflict. The anticipation of defensiveness or misunderstandings can paralyze us, making it challenging to articulate our feelings authentically. It's as if we're walking on eggshells, afraid that any misstep could trigger a negative response.

Additionally, the fear that our perspective won't be understood or valued adds another layer of complexity. We grapple with doubts about our ability to convey our emotions effectively and fear the consequences of being misunderstood or dismissed. This fear of not being heard or validated heightens our vulnerability, further inhibiting our willingness to engage in these challenging conversations. Thus, the fear of confrontation and the uncertainty of being understood create a huge barrier to open and honest communication.

Conversations become even more challenging when addiction is involved, primarily due to the profound impact addiction has on communication dynamics. Addiction alters the very fabric of interpersonal interactions, creating a tangled web of denial, defensiveness, and mistrust. The person struggling with addiction may be entrenched in denial, unable or unwilling to acknowledge the severity of their behavior. This denial serves as a protective shield, shielding them from the harsh reality of their actions and deflecting any attempts at intervention or confrontation.

Moreover, addiction breeds defensiveness, as individuals often feel attacked or judged when their behaviors are called into question. They may perceive any discussion about their addiction as a personal attack, leading to heightened tensions and emotional volatility. This defensiveness further complicates communication, making it akin to navigating a treacherous minefield where every word has the potential to detonate explosive emotions.

In this hostile terrain, even well-intentioned conversations can backfire, exacerbating conflicts and driving a deeper wedge between individuals. The fear of triggering the person struggling with addiction looms large, casting a shadow of uncertainty over every interaction. As a result, communication becomes fraught with anxiety and apprehension, hindering the possibility of meaningful dialogue and resolution.

Instead of bottling up our emotions, it is essential to cultivate healthy ways of expressing and managing them. This may involve practicing mindfulness, journaling, seeking support from trusted friends or professionals, engaging in creative outlets such as art or music, or simply allowing ourselves to feel our emotions without judgment. By acknowledging and honoring our feelings, we can prevent the pressure cooker effect and maintain emotional well-being, leading to a more balanced and fulfilling life.

Empowering Responsive Communication and Release the Pressure Valve

When we bottle up our emotions, we inadvertently set ourselves up for a reactive rather than a responsive mode of interaction. Bottling up emotions essentially means suppressing or avoiding our feelings, needs, and inner voice in the context of our loved one's addiction struggles, which can lead to a buildup of tension and pressure over time. This internal pressure creates a volatile emotional state where even minor triggers can provoke intense reactions.

In a reactive state, we tend to respond impulsively and emotionally to situations related to our loved one's addiction without taking the time to reflect on our true feelings and needs. Instead of responding thoughtfully and intentionally, we react based on our immediate emotional state, which may be clouded by pent-up frustration, resentment, or fear.

Reacting in this manner often triggers a cycle of escalating conflicts, misunderstandings, and hurt feelings within the relationship. Our responses are fueled by intense emotions simmering beneath the surface, leading us to lash out defensively, say hurtful things, or withdraw altogether. These reactions contribute to communication breakdowns and deepen relational tensions, especially when dealing with a loved one struggling with addiction.

Moreover, the individual grappling with addiction may employ manipulation tactics to provoke explosive responses. This manipulation, often seen as gaslighting, aims to deflect attention from the underlying issue of addiction by making the other person appear irrational or unstable. As a result, the focus shifts away from addressing the root cause, further complicating the communication dynamic and perpetuating the cycle of conflict.

On the other hand, when we take the time to process and work with our emotions, needs, and inner voice within the context of our loved one's addiction, we cultivate a more responsive approach to interactions. This involves acknowledging and expressing our feelings in a healthy and constructive manner, rather than bottling them up or letting them explode. This shift of dynamic where you become responsive instead of reactive brings you strength and power.

By tuning into our inner workings and gaining clarity on our emotions, needs, and boundaries within the context of addiction, we empower ourselves to respond thoughtfully and authentically to challenging situations. Instead of reacting impulsively from a place of emotional turmoil, we can pause, reflect, and choose how we want to engage with our loved one and the addiction dynamic.

Responsive communication allows us to express ourselves assertively yet respectfully, advocating for our needs while also considering the perspectives and feelings of our loved one. It fosters deeper understanding, empathy, and connection in our relationship, as we engage in meaningful dialogue and mutual problem-solving.

Moreover, cultivating responsiveness within the context of loving someone with an addiction enables us to reclaim our personal power and agency in interactions, rather than feeling at the mercy of our volatile emotions. We become active participants in shaping the dynamics of our relationship with our loved one and the addiction, rather than passive reactors to external stimuli.

In essence, by processing our emotions, needs, and inner voice within the context of our loved one's addiction, we can transcend reactive patterns and cultivate a more empowered and authentic way of engaging with the situation. This shift from reaction to response empowers us to navigate our relationship with greater wisdom, self-compassion, and integrity, fostering deeper connection and emotional well-being amidst the complexities of loving someone with an addiction.

Staying Grounded Amidst Chaos

Navigating the rollercoaster of emotions while loving someone with addiction can feel like a wild ride, leaving us wondering how to honor our own feelings and needs without bottling them up. Staying responsive instead of reactive is key, but it's easier said than done, especially when their actions leave us feeling like we're losing our minds.

So, how do we honor our emotions and needs in the midst of chaos?

It starts with acknowledging that our feelings are valid, even when they seem overwhelming or irrational. Instead of stuffing them down or pretending they don't exist, we can give ourselves permission to feel them fully.

But here's the tricky part: when our loved one's behavior pushes all our buttons, it's tempting to react impulsively. We might snap back defensively, retreat into silence, or explode in frustration. However, reacting in the heat of the moment only adds fuel to the fire, escalating conflicts and leaving both parties feeling even more disconnected.

Instead, staying responsive means taking a step back and tuning into our inner voice. It's about recognizing our emotions without letting them dictate our actions. By creating space to process our feelings, we can respond thoughtfully rather than impulsively. This might involve taking a deep breath, seeking a moment of solitude, or journaling to gain clarity.

But how does this help us navigate the tough decision of whether to stay or go?

By staying responsive, we empower ourselves to make decisions from a place of clarity and self-awareness rather than reactive emotion. We can weigh the pros and cons of our relationship with a clear head, considering our own well-being and values alongside the challenges we face.

In essence, honoring our emotions and needs while staying responsive allows us to reclaim our power in the face of adversity. It's a journey of self-discovery and empowerment that enables us to navigate tough relationship decisions with grace and integrity, no matter how crazy things may seem.

Navigating the Internal Dialogue: Cultivating Self-Compassion and Inner Nurturance

If only you could read my mind, you'd probably hear a chorus of critical voices echoing inside. It's something many of us experience—the constant stream of self-criticism that can be as relentless as it is unkind. We often convince ourselves that by being tough on ourselves, we'll somehow motivate change or spur ourselves into action. But the truth is, being harsh only adds to our burden.

Have you ever noticed that voice inside your head—the one that seems to pick apart every decision, every action, every flaw? That's your inner critic at work, and let me tell you, it can be ruthless. It's the voice that whispers you're not good enough, you'll never measure up, you're a failure. And with every negative word, it chips away at our self-esteem, leaving us feeling small and unworthy.

In times of turmoil, when we're already grappling with so much, the last thing we need is to turn on ourselves. Yet, I'll admit, I've had my fair share of moments where I've berated myself, questioning my intelligence, my worth, my choices. The sting of those self-inflicted wounds—words like "stupid" or "idiot"—can cut deep, leaving us reeling with self-doubt and regret. Ouch.

What we really need is an inner nurturer—a compassionate voice that speaks to us with kindness and understanding. Instead of berating ourselves for our situations, our inner nurturer offers words of encouragement and support. It reminds us that we're only human, that it's okay to make mistakes, and that we're worthy of love and acceptance just as we are.

Connecting with our emotions is a crucial part of this process. When we allow ourselves to feel our emotions fully, without judgment or criticism, we create space for healing and authenticity. Emotions are like messengers, carrying important information about our innermost needs and desires. By tuning into these emotions and acknowledging them with compassion, we can begin to understand ourselves on a deeper level and live more authentically.

Practicing self-compassion around our emotions is empowering because it allows us to embrace our humanity fully. Instead of seeing our emotions as weaknesses to be suppressed or ignored, we recognize them as valid and worthy of our attention. This shift in perspective frees us from the grip of our inner critic and empowers us to live with greater authenticity and self-acceptance.

Why is all of this important when navigating a relationship touched by addiction?

Because addiction thrives in secrecy and shame. When we're caught up in our inner critic's negative narrative, we're more likely to hide our struggles and isolate ourselves from others. But when we cultivate self-compassion and inner nurturance, we create a safe space within ourselves where we can acknowledge our pain and seek support from others.

In a relationship affected by addiction, this inner work becomes even more crucial. It enables us to set boundaries, communicate assertively, and advocate for our own needs. By nurturing ourselves from the inside out, we become better equipped to navigate the challenges of addiction with grace and resilience.

If You Could Read My Mind: An Inner Dialogue Exercise

Take a moment to engage in this inner dialogue exercise and observe the empowering feeling that comes from honoring our internal conversations while enhancing self-awareness.

Instructions:
1. Find a quiet and comfortable space where you won't be interrupted.

2. Take a few deep breaths to center yourself and quiet your mind.

3. Close your eyes and imagine a scenario where you're facing a challenging situation or decision related to your loved one's addiction.

4. Allow yourself to become aware of the thoughts and emotions that arise within you. Notice any self-critical or negative thoughts that may surface, as well as any intuitive feelings or inner guidance.

5. Imagine that you're having a conversation with your inner critic. Write down the negative thoughts and criticisms it's expressing towards you.

6. Then, imagine inviting your inner nurturer into the conversation. Write down the compassionate and supportive responses it offers in response to your inner critic's criticisms.

7. Take a moment to reflect on the dialogue between your inner critic and inner nurturer. Notice how each voice makes you feel and how it influences your perception of the situation.

8. Now, tune into your emotions. Notice any feelings of fear, doubt, or uncertainty that may be present. Allow yourself to fully experience these emotions without judgment.

9. Finally, tap into your intuition and inner wisdom. Ask yourself what feels right and true for you in this situation. Trust your gut instincts and listen to the inner guidance that arises within you.

10. Write down any insights or revelations that come to you during this exercise.

Reflection:
After completing the exercise, take some time to reflect on what you've discovered about yourself and your inner dialogue. Notice any patterns or recurring themes in your thoughts, emotions, and intuitive guidance. Consider how you can cultivate more self-compassion and nurturing towards yourself in moments of self-doubt or criticism. Use this exercise as a tool to deepen your understanding of your internal landscape and strengthen your connection to your intuition and inner wisdom.

Self-Compassion: Nurturing Yourself Through Difficult Times

Have you ever struggled to extend the same compassion to yourself that you readily offer to others during challenging times?

Self-compassion, a concept pioneered by psychologist Kristin Neff, refers to the practice of treating oneself with kindness, understanding, and acceptance, especially during moments of struggle or suffering.

It involves recognizing one's own humanity, acknowledging personal flaws and imperfections, and offering oneself the same compassion and support that one would extend to a friend in a similar situation.

In the context of relationships affected by addiction, self-compassion is particularly vital. The challenges and complexities of loving someone with an addiction can take a significant toll on one's emotional well-being. In such situations, self-compassion serves as a vital tool for maintaining resilience, preserving self-worth, and navigating the inevitable ups and downs with grace and understanding.

Self-compassion can help individuals while navigating tough relationship decisions by providing a supportive and nurturing inner dialogue. Instead of succumbing to self-criticism or harsh judgment, individuals can practice self-compassion by acknowledging their own pain and difficulties with kindness and empathy. This gentle approach fosters emotional resilience and clarity, enabling individuals to make decisions from a place of self-awareness and self-care.

To be kind to yourself amidst the challenges of loving someone with an addiction, it's essential to cultivate a practice of self-compassion. This involves:

Self-Awareness: Recognize when you're being self-critical or judgmental, and consciously choose to shift towards a more compassionate mindset.

Self-Kindness: Treat yourself with the same kindness and understanding that you would offer to a loved one facing similar struggles. Offer words of encouragement and support to yourself, acknowledging your efforts and strengths.

Mindfulness: Practice mindfulness techniques to stay present and grounded in the moment, allowing yourself to observe your thoughts and emotions without judgment.

Self-Validation: Validate your own experiences and feelings, recognizing that they are valid and worthy of acknowledgment and acceptance.

To cultivate fierce self-compassion, consider practicing the following exercise:

Compassionate Self-Talk Exercise

- Find a quiet and comfortable space where you can sit or lie down comfortably.

- Close your eyes and take several deep breaths, allowing yourself to relax and center your attention inward.

- Bring to mind a recent challenging situation or decision you've faced in your relationship affected by addiction.

- Imagine yourself as a compassionate and supportive friend, offering words of comfort and encouragement to yourself.

- Speak to yourself with kindness and understanding, acknowledging the difficulty of the situation and offering reassurance that you're doing the best you can.

- Repeat compassionate phrases such as, "It's okay to feel overwhelmed," "You're not alone in this," and "You're doing the best you can with the resources you have."

- Continue this practice for several minutes, allowing yourself to fully embrace the warmth and comfort of your own self-compassion.

By incorporating self-compassion into your journey of navigating tough relationship decisions, you can cultivate greater resilience, inner strength, and well-being. Remember that loving someone with an addiction can be incredibly challenging, and practicing self-compassion is essential for preserving your emotional health and finding peace amidst the storm.

To Summarize

In the end, if we could peer into your mind, understanding the significance of honoring our emotions, needs, and inner struggles would be crystal clear. It's about meeting ourselves with love and compassion, acknowledging the battles we may be fighting within. But it's also about confronting that inner voice—the one that whispers doubts and insecurities—with honesty and courage.

Navigating the emotional whirlwind of a relationship touched by addiction requires us to dig deep and confront our inner turmoil head-on. It's about recognizing when our emotions are bubbling to the surface, when our needs aren't being met, and when our values are being compromised. And it's about safeguarding our mental health along the way, treating ourselves with the kindness and respect we deserve.

In this journey, tapping into our inner nurturer becomes essential—a gentle guide that leads us through the storms with grace and compassion. From this place of empowerment and self-awareness, we can take meaningful action, even if it means starting with small, steps toward what truly matters to us. Ultimately, it's about honoring ourselves, respecting our journey, and moving forward with confidence and authenticity.

Key Insights

Trusting Your Inner Voice: Listening to your intuition and engaging in self-reflection are vital for navigating relationships authentically. By tuning into subtle cues and trusting your inner voice, you can make decisions aligned with your values. Practices like journaling and mindfulness empower you to uncover hidden patterns and deepen connections.

Honoring Your Values: Staying true to your values is essential for fulfillment in life and relationships. Reflecting on core values like honesty and compassion guides your actions and provides clarity for the future. Aligning decisions with your values cultivates relationships reflecting your true essence, fostering happiness.

Navigating Emotional Turmoil: Embracing self-compassion and honoring emotions is crucial for navigating complexities, especially in addiction-affected relationships. Tuning into your inner voice, processing feelings, and making well-being-aligned decisions reclaim your power, fostering understanding and connection.

Navigating the Internal Dialogue: Cultivating self-compassion amid inner criticism, especially in addiction-affected relationships, is vital. By nurturing an inner voice of kindness and connecting with emotions, you empower yourself to navigate challenges with authenticity and resilience.

Cultivating Self-Compassion: Self-compassion is key during challenging times like navigating addiction-affected relationships. Treating yourself with kindness and acceptance, akin to supporting a friend, preserves self-worth and resilience, guiding decisions from a place of clarity and care.

Consolidating Our Insights: Trusting our instincts and listening to our inner voice is essential when making tough relationship decisions, especially in relationships affected by addiction. Our intuition often offers valuable guidance beyond logical reasoning, helping us navigate complex situations with clarity and authenticity.

Honoring our values and staying true to what is important to us is crucial for decision-making. By aligning our choices with our values, we ensure that our decisions are authentic and reflective of our deepest desires and aspirations.

Being aware of our inner dialogue allows us to identify and address any conflicting thoughts or emotions that may arise during the decision-making process. Understanding and practicing self-compassion are also essential, as they enable us to approach tough decisions with kindness and understanding, fostering resilience and emotional well-being.

Our inner nurturing voice plays a significant role in decision-making, offering us comfort, encouragement, and guidance as we navigate challenging situations. Practicing self-compassion during times of uncertainty and doubt can help us navigate tough decisions with grace and self-assurance.

> **Reflection:** *Reflecting on the insights shared about trusting your instincts and honoring your values, consider the following questions: How do you typically approach tough relationship decisions? Do you tend to rely more on logical reasoning or your intuition? How do your values influence your decision-making process? Have you ever experienced conflicting thoughts or emotions when making tough decisions, and if so, how did you address them? In what ways do you practice self-compassion during times of uncertainty and doubt? Finally, how does your inner nurturing voice support you in navigating challenging situations?*

CHAPTER 8

PUTTING MY OXYGEN MASK ON

Affirming Your Value and Empowering Your Path Forward

Introduction

In the journey of loving someone with addiction, it's easy to get lost in the chaos and neglect our own well-being. We often find ourselves putting the needs of our loved ones before our own, leaving little time or energy for self-care. However, as the saying goes, you can't pour from an empty cup. In this chapter, titled "Putting My Oxygen Mask On: Affirming Your Value and Empowering Your Path Forward," we'll explore the crucial importance of self-care in preserving your well-being and navigating relationships affected by addiction's shadow.

Throughout this entire book, the emphasis has been on the significance of prioritizing self-care as a means of self-preservation and resilience. Each chapter has been a step along the journey of nurturing yourself and safeguarding your mental health while navigating tough relationship decisions. In this chapter, we will dig a little deeper into self-care, community, and courage.

Positive psychology highlights the profound impact of self-care on our psychological resilience and vitality. By investing in self-care practices, we enhance our ability to cope with stress, cultivate positive emotions, and maintain a sense of meaning and purpose in life. Self-care equips us with the necessary tools to navigate challenges, make decisions aligned with our values, and foster fulfilling relationships, even amidst the complexities of addiction.

From embracing community support to crafting a vision for your future, let's explore various facets of self-care that contribute to overall well-being and happiness.

As we delve into the chapters ahead, we'll explore empowering narratives, courageously envisioning our future selves, and embracing hope amidst the darkness of addiction's shadow. Together, let's reaffirm our value, prioritize our well-being, and empower our path forward by putting our oxygen masks on first.

Prioritizing Self-Care: Nurturing Your Well-Being

Do you struggle to prioritize yourself and carve out time for self-care, especially when faced with the demanding effects that come with loving someone dealing with addiction?

Self-care isn't just about indulging in spa days or bubble baths; it's about intentionally tending to your physical, emotional, and mental needs. In a relationship touched by addiction, self-care takes on added significance. The stress, uncertainty, and emotional turmoil can easily deplete your reserves, making it essential to replenish and rejuvenate yourself regularly.

In the midst of navigating tough relationship decisions and the complexities of loving someone with addiction, prioritizing self-care becomes not just important but essential for maintaining your overall well-being and emotional health. Here are some key ways to commit to self-care and nurture yourself through these challenging circumstances:

The 'How To' Of Self-Care

Throughout this book, the overarching theme has been preserving your well-being and safeguarding your mental health. You may have noticed that each chapter has been a step along the journey of self-care and self-preservation.

Here, we emphasize the significance of self-care by exploring its importance and offering practical strategies for integrating it into your daily routine.

Acknowledge Your Needs: Start by recognizing and acknowledging your own needs, both physical and emotional. Understand that it's okay to prioritize yourself and your well-being, even amidst the chaos of addiction

Set Boundaries: Establishing healthy boundaries is crucial for protecting your mental and emotional health. This may involve setting limits on the time and energy you devote to supporting your loved one, as well as asserting boundaries around behaviors that are harmful or toxic to you.

Seek Support: Don't hesitate to reach out for support from friends, family members, support groups, or mental health professionals.

Surround yourself with a supportive network of individuals who can offer guidance, empathy, and understanding as you navigate these difficult decisions.

Practice Self-Compassion: Be gentle with yourself and practice self-compassion as you navigate the challenges of loving someone with addiction. Recognize that it's okay to feel overwhelmed, and give yourself permission to experience a range of emotions without judgment.

Engage in Self-Care Activities: Dedicate time to engage in activities that nourish your mind, body, and soul. This may include exercise, meditation, journaling, spending time in nature, or indulging in hobbies that bring you joy and relaxation.

Prioritize Your Physical Health: Taking care of your physical health is just as important as tending to your emotional well-being. Make sure to prioritize activities such as eating nutritious meals, getting regular exercise, staying hydrated, and getting enough sleep.

Practice Mindfulness: Cultivate mindfulness practices to help you stay grounded and present in the moment. Mindfulness techniques such as deep breathing, meditation, or mindfulness exercises can help reduce stress and promote emotional balance.

Set Realistic Expectations: Be realistic about what you can and cannot control in the situation. Understand that you cannot force your loved one to change their behavior, and focus instead on what you can do to take care of yourself and make healthy decisions for your own well-being.

By committing to self-care and prioritizing your well-being, you empower yourself to navigate tough relationship decisions with clarity, resilience, and compassion. Remember that taking care of yourself is not selfish, but rather an essential aspect of maintaining your overall health and happiness, even in the face of addiction-related challenges.

Self-Care For Self-Preservation and Resilience

Positive psychology underscores the importance of self-care in promoting overall well-being and happiness. When you prioritize self-care, you're investing in your long-term psychological resilience and vitality. Self-care practices enhance your ability to cope with stress, cultivate positive emotions, and maintain a sense of meaning and purpose in life. By nurturing yourself, you're better equipped to navigate challenges, make decisions aligned with your values, and foster fulfilling relationships.

Committing to self-care is not selfish; it's an act of self-preservation and empowerment. By prioritizing your well-being amidst the complexities of loving someone with an addiction, you honor your inherent worth and strengthen your capacity to navigate tough relationship decisions with grace and clarity. Remember, taking care of yourself isn't a luxury—it's a necessity for a thriving, fulfilling life.

Self-Care For Managing Stress and Building Resilience

Chronic stress can have profound effects on both the body and mind, significantly impacting our overall well-being. When we love someone with addiction, the constant worry, uncertainty, and emotional turmoil can contribute to chronic stress, further exacerbating our physical and mental health.

Chronic stress can manifest physically in various ways, including increased blood pressure, elevated heart rate, muscle tension, and weakened immune function. Over time, these physiological changes can lead to a range of health issues, such as cardiovascular disease, digestive problems, and immune disorders.

On a psychological level, chronic stress can take a toll on our mental health, leading to symptoms such as anxiety, depression, irritability, and difficulty concentrating. It can also contribute to feelings of overwhelm, burnout, and emotional exhaustion.

Given the significant impact of chronic stress on our well-being, it becomes essential to prioritize self-care as a means of managing and mitigating its effects. Self-care practices provide us with the tools and strategies to cope with stress effectively, promoting resilience, emotional balance, and overall wellness.

Four categories of self-care practices that can be particularly beneficial for dealing with stress:

Physical Self-Care involves activities that nourish and support physical health. Examples include regular exercise, getting enough sleep, maintaining a balanced diet, staying hydrated, and practicing relaxation techniques such as deep breathing or progressive muscle relaxation.

Emotional Self-Care: Emotional self-care focuses on nurturing our emotional well-being and cultivating resilience in the face of stress.

This may involve practices such as journaling, expressing emotions through creative outlets like art or music, seeking support from friends or a therapist, practicing self-compassion and mindfulness, and setting boundaries to protect our emotional energy.

Social Self-Care: Social connections are essential for buffering the effects of stress and promoting overall well-being. Engaging in meaningful relationships, spending time with supportive friends and family members, participating in group activities or support groups, and seeking out opportunities for social connection and belonging can all contribute to emotional resilience and stress management.

Spiritual Self-Care: Spiritual self-care involves nurturing our sense of purpose, meaning, and connection to something greater than ourselves. This may include practices such as meditation, prayer, spending time in nature, engaging in acts of kindness and service, reflecting on our values and beliefs, and cultivating gratitude and mindfulness in daily life.

By incorporating these self-care practices into our daily routine, we can effectively manage the impact of chronic stress and promote our overall well-being. Remember that self-care is an essential aspect of maintaining resilience, vitality, and balance, especially when navigating the challenges of loving someone with addiction.

Reflecting on the impact of chronic stress in your own life, what self-care practices have you found most effective in managing stress and promoting resilience? How can you incorporate these practices into your daily routine to prioritize your well-being?

Embracing Community: Finding Support Amidst Relationships Affected by Addiction's Shadow

Who in your life do you feel has your back when it comes to navigating the challenges of relationships affected by addiction? Additionally, are there any other places or communities where you feel a sense of connectedness and support?

In the journey of loving someone with addiction, the importance of human connection cannot be overstated. It's natural to feel isolated amidst the complexities and challenges this situation brings. Loving an addict can be an incredibly lonely experience. You may find yourself grappling with emotions, uncertainties, and difficulties that others may not fully understand. This sense of isolation can exacerbate feelings of despair, anxiety, and overwhelm, posing significant dangers to your emotional well-being.

However, it's crucial to recognize that you're not alone in this journey. Finding connection and support from others who understand your experiences can provide immense comfort and strength. Befriending individuals who share similar challenges or joining communities dedicated to supporting the loved ones of addicts can offer a lifeline during times of struggle.

Sources of connection in navigating relationships affected by addiction's shadow can include

Support Groups: Joining support groups specifically tailored to the loved ones of individuals with addiction can provide a sense of belonging and understanding. These groups offer opportunities to share experiences, receive support, and gain insights from others who are going through similar challenges.

Therapeutic Services: Seeking therapy or counseling can offer a supportive and non-judgmental space to explore your feelings, gain clarity, and develop coping strategies. Therapists specializing in addiction or family therapy can provide valuable guidance and support in navigating relationship dynamics impacted by addiction.

Online Communities: Participating in online communities, forums, or social media groups dedicated to supporting loved ones of individuals with addiction can be a convenient way to connect with others facing similar struggles. These platforms allow for sharing experiences, exchanging advice, and finding solidarity with others who understand your situation.

Educational Resources: Engaging with educational resources such as books, articles, podcasts, or workshops on addiction and relationships can provide valuable insights and tools for navigating challenges. Learning about addiction, boundaries, communication strategies, and self-care practices can empower individuals to better understand their experiences and make informed decisions.

Family and Friends: Building and maintaining connections with supportive friends and family members can offer emotional support and practical assistance in times of need. Having trusted individuals to lean on and confide in can provide comfort and validation while navigating the complexities of relationships affected by addiction.

Community Organizations: Getting involved with local community organizations or advocacy groups focused on addiction awareness and support can offer opportunities for connection, volunteerism, and collective action. These organizations often host events, meetings, or activities where individuals can connect with others passionate about supporting those impacted by addiction.

By embracing these sources of connection, individuals can find support, understanding, and encouragement as they navigate relationships affected by addiction's shadow. These connections can offer valuable insights, validation, and companionship on the journey towards healing and recovery.

Through these connections, you'll discover a sense of belonging and understanding that can alleviate feelings of isolation and loneliness. Whether it's through online forums, support groups, or local community organizations, reaching out to others who are navigating similar paths can offer invaluable empathy, guidance, and solidarity.

A Personal Invitation to S.Y.K.M.

Join the Saving You Is Killing Me (S.Y.K.M.) Community, a supportive space created for individuals who understand the unique struggles of loving someone with addiction. Our inclusive platform offers a range of resources, including a website, podcast, and Facebook group, where members can connect, share experiences, and find solace. Whether you're seeking practical advice, emotional support, or simply a listening ear, our community provides a safe and compassionate environment to navigate the challenges of loving someone with addiction. You are not alone—we are here for you every step of the way.

By embracing community and fostering meaningful connections, you can find solace, strength, and resilience in the midst of adversity. Together, we can support each other, share our stories, and journey towards healing and hope. Remember, you are not alone—there is a community waiting to welcome you with open arms and walk alongside you every step of the way.

Courage: Crafting a Vision for Your Future

What dreams or aspirations do you hold for your future if addiction weren't a factor influencing your path?

Courage in relationships refers to the ability to face challenges, uncertainties, and vulnerabilities with bravery and resilience. It involves taking proactive steps to navigate difficult situations, confront fears, and pursue growth and fulfillment in relationships. Courage is not the absence of fear but rather the willingness to act in spite of fear, discomfort, or uncertainty, driven by a sense of purpose and values. Courage is about knowing your worth and worthiness for a life that feels good.

Courage is the cornerstone of growth and transformation in relationships. It's not just about facing external challenges but also about having the strength to prioritize your own well-being and happiness, even in the face of adversity. In the context of relationships affected by addiction, courage means having the resilience to focus on yourself and your own growth, independent of your loved one's struggles.

It's important to recognize that your happiness and fulfillment are not dependent on the actions or behaviors of your loved one with addiction. You have the power to create a fulfilling life for yourself, regardless of the circumstances around you. This requires the courage to set boundaries, prioritize self-care, and pursue your own goals and aspirations.

With courage as your guide, you can establish personal and relationship goals with confidence. Take the time to envision the future you desire, both for yourself and for your relationship, and then take proactive steps to make that vision a reality.

Consider asking yourself: Who do you want to be in your relationships and in your life? What values do you want to embody, and what strengths do you want to cultivate? By clarifying your aspirations and values, you can set goals that resonate deeply with you and contribute to your overall well-being and happiness.

Courageous Compassion: Navigating Relationships Touched by Addiction through Love Lists

Courage is found in our ability to be truthful with ourselves, acknowledging the qualities and attributes we desire in a relationship. One effective tool that has greatly aided me in navigating challenging relationship decisions is creating a "Love List." This comprehensive list comprises all the qualities and characteristics I value in a potential partner. While you may already be in a relationship, crafting a Love List without attaching it to a specific person allows you to recognize what truly matters to you and what you seek in a partnership. This list serves as a benchmark, enabling you to compare your current relationship against your authentic desires. Alternatively, you can create a "Value List" by considering the qualities and attributes you bring to a relationship. Reflecting on your own strengths and contributions can be empowering, bolstering your courage and fortitude as you navigate the complexities of love and partnership.

Creating Your Love List

Instructions for Creating Your Love List

Begin by Brain Dumping: Take some time to brainstorm and jot down all the qualities and characteristics that you value in a relationship. Consider past relationships, aspects you enjoy in your current relationship, and anything else that comes to mind. Don't censor yourself; let your thoughts flow freely.

Capture What Matters: Include everything that matters to you in a relationship, whether it's morning snuggles, working out together, or deep conversations. The goal is to capture what brings you joy and fulfillment in a partnership to you.

Choose Your Format: You can create your Love List on a big Bristol board, in a journal, or as a mind map. If using a mind map, start with a central theme like "Ideal Partner" and branch out with related qualities and characteristics.

Get Specific: Dive deep into what you're looking for in a partner. If you value confidence, for example, consider related traits like humility, initiative, or engaging in conversation.

Use Colors and Creativity: Feel free to use different colors and creative elements to make your Love List visually appealing. This will help you engage with it and make it more meaningful.

Include Inspirations: If you have friends or acquaintances whose relationships you admire, consider including qualities from those partnerships in your Love List.

All About You, My Self Love List

Instructions for Creating Your All About My Self Love List

Create a Love List for Yourself: Once you've completed your Love List for your ideal partner, turn the focus inward and create a second Love List for yourself. Write down all the qualities and characteristics that you bring to a relationship. Take the time you deserve. See your value and your worth.

Reflect and Review: Take some time to reflect on your Love Lists and consider how they align with your desires and values. Use them as a guide as you navigate your relationships and strive for personal growth and fulfillment.

The Power of Love Lists in Navigating Addiction: Creating a Love List encompassing both qualities we seek in an ideal partner and those we bring to relationships is a courageous act rooted in self-awareness and authenticity. It requires honesty with ourselves as we acknowledge our desires, strengths, and areas for growth. By bravely confronting our inner truths, we empower ourselves to navigate relationships with clarity and intentionality.

Tapping into our courage means facing our vulnerabilities and expressing our authentic selves. When we compile a Love List for an ideal partner, we're acknowledging our deepest desires and values in a relationship. This honesty allows us to set clear boundaries and expectations, ensuring that we pursue connections that align with our true selves.

Similarly, creating a Love List for ourselves highlights our unique qualities and contributions to relationships. It takes courage to recognize and celebrate our strengths. By embracing our worth and value, we cultivate self-confidence and resilience, which are essential for building healthy and fulfilling connections.

Having these Love Lists serves as a compass in our relationship journey, guiding us toward partnerships that honor our values and aspirations. When we communicate our needs and expectations openly and honestly, we set the stage for meaningful connections built on mutual respect and understanding. Moreover, knowing what we bring to relationships empowers us to enter into connections confidently, knowing that we have much to offer and deserve to be valued for who we are.

In essence, creating Love Lists requires us to step into our courage, confront our truths, and advocate for our needs and desires. By doing so, we cultivate deeper self-awareness, authenticity, and empowerment, which are invaluable assets as we navigate the complexities of relationships with confidence and clarity.

Navigating a relationship affected by addiction amplifies the need for courage and self-awareness in creating Love Lists for both an ideal partner and ourselves. When loving someone with addiction, the challenges and complexities can often overshadow our own needs and desires. However, it's precisely in these situations that having clarity about what we seek in a relationship and what we bring to it becomes crucial.

Being in a relationship touched by addiction, the journey can be emotionally taxing and uncertain. Creating a Love List allows us to articulate the qualities and values we seek in a partner, providing a beacon of hope and direction amidst the chaos. It empowers us to establish personal boundaries, as well as limits and advocate for our well-being, even in the face of addiction-related challenges.

Similarly, compiling a Love List for ourselves reaffirms our worth and value, which can easily be eroded in the tumult of addiction. By recognizing our strengths and contributions to relationships, we bolster our resilience and self-esteem, essential qualities for navigating the ups and downs of loving someone with addiction.

Having these Love Lists helps us stay grounded in our truth and authenticity, even as we confront the complexities of addiction. They serve as reminders of our priorities, values, and aspirations, guiding us in making decisions that honor our well-being and align with our long-term goals.

In essence, creating Love Lists in the context of a relationship touched by addiction is an act of self-preservation and empowerment. It enables us to navigate the challenges with clarity, resilience, and self-assurance, ultimately fostering healthier and more fulfilling connections amidst adversity.

Courageous Vision: Crafting Your Future Self Amidst Relationship Challenges

In the midst of relationship challenges, maintaining clarity of purpose and goals can be a beacon of light guiding us forward. By setting clear intentions and aligning them with our values and strengths, we empower ourselves to make decisions that resonate with our deepest desires. In this section, we delve into the transformative power of visualization and goal-setting exercises, offering practical tools to help navigate the complexities of relationships affected by addiction. Through the Future Self Visualization and Goal Setting Exercise, we go on a journey of self-discovery and empowerment, forging a path toward our ideal future amidst adversity. Let's explore how these practices can cultivate courage, resilience, and clarity as we navigate the terrain of love and addiction.

 **Crafting Your Future Self Amidst Relationship Challenges Exercise**

In the face of adversity, it takes courage to envision a brighter future and take proactive steps toward it. This exercise encourages you to connect with your future self, identify your aspirations, and set actionable goals that align with your vision. Here's how to get started:

Connect with Your Future Self:
Begin by finding a quiet and comfortable space where you can focus without distractions. Close your eyes and visualize meeting your future self—the person you aspire to become. Imagine living a life filled with fulfillment, purpose, and joy. Notice the qualities, achievements, and experiences that define your future self. Allow yourself to connect deeply with this vision, embracing the emotions and sensations it evokes.

Identify Your Aspirations:
Reflect on the aspirations and goals that resonate with your future self. What do you hope to accomplish or experience in your life? Consider different areas such as personal growth, relationships, career, health, and well-being. Write down your aspirations in a journal or notebook, allowing yourself to explore and articulate your deepest desires.

Set Future Self Goals:
Transform your aspirations into SMART goals: Specific, Measurable, Achievable, Relevant, and Time-bound. Break down your goals into actionable steps that you can take to manifest your future self. Write down each goal and its corresponding action plan, focusing on concrete steps you can take to move closer to your vision.

Create a Vision of Success:
Visualize yourself achieving your goals and embodying your future self. Picture the details of what success looks and feels like to you. Use your imagination to create a vivid mental image of your ideal future, focusing on the positive emotions and sensations associated with accomplishing your goals.

Create a Vision Board:
From your visualization and vision, take the time to create a visual representation that supports your future self. Gather materials such as poster board or corkboard, magazines, scissors, glue, markers, and decorative items. Reflect on the images, words, and symbols that resonate with the vision you've visualized during the exercise, representing your goals, values, aspirations, or desired feelings. Cut out the ones that resonate and evoke the emotions associated with your ideal future, arranging them on your board in a meaningful way.

Develop a Future Self Action Plan:
Based on your goals and vision of success, create a future self action plan. Identify the specific actions, habits, and behaviors that will support your journey towards becoming your future self. Break down your action plan into daily, weekly, and monthly tasks, setting yourself up for success.

Practice Visualization and Affirmations:
Incorporate visualization and positive affirmations into your daily routine to reinforce your connection with your future self and goals. Spend a few minutes each day visualizing yourself achieving your goals and affirming your ability to manifest your aspirations. Use empowering statements such as "I am capable of achieving my dreams" and "I am worthy of success and fulfillment."

Review and Revise Regularly:
Regularly review your goals and action plan to track your progress and stay motivated. Reflect on the steps you've taken towards your future self and celebrate your achievements along the way. Adjust your goals and action plan as needed, staying flexible and adaptable to changes in your circumstances or priorities.

By engaging in this exercise, you cultivate the courage to envision a future filled with hope and possibility, despite the challenges you may face. You empower yourself to take proactive steps towards your ideal future, guided by decisions that resonate with your values, strengths, and dreams. As you continue on this journey of self-discovery and empowerment, remember that the power to shape your destiny lies within you. Embrace the courage to craft your future self amidst relationship challenges, and watch as your vision unfolds before your eyes.

Empowering Narratives: Embracing Hope Amidst Addiction's Shadow

Our narratives shape how we perceive ourselves and the world, influencing our beliefs, attitudes, and actions. When faced with the challenges of loving someone with addiction, it's easy to adopt a victim mentality, feeling powerless and overwhelmed. However, we have the power to rewrite our narrative and become the hero of our own story. By embracing empowering narratives, we can reclaim our agency, cultivate hope, and navigate relationships with strength and resilience.

Embracing Empowering Narratives: Becoming the Hero of Your Own Story

Narratives shape the way we perceive ourselves and the world around us. They influence our beliefs, attitudes, and behaviors, often serving as powerful determinants of our experiences and outcomes. In the context of loving someone with addiction, it's easy to fall into the role of the victim, feeling powerless and overwhelmed by circumstances. However, we have the power to rewrite our narrative and step into the role of the hero in our own story. By embracing a narrative framework where we are the powerful hero overcoming challenges with resilience and courage, we can reclaim our agency, cultivate hope, and empower ourselves to navigate the complexities of loving someone with addiction.

Exploring the Power of Narrative
At its core, narrative refers to the stories we tell ourselves about who we are, where we come from, and what we're capable of achieving. These stories shape our perceptions of reality, influencing how we interpret events, make sense of our experiences, and navigate the world around us. When faced with challenges like loving someone with addiction, our narrative can either empower us or constrain us, depending on how we choose to frame our experiences.

Changing Your Narrative: From Victim to Hero
The first step in changing your narrative is to recognize that you have the power to do so. Instead of seeing yourself as a passive victim of

circumstances, embrace a narrative framework where you are the hero of your own story. Identify your strengths, confront difficulties with resilience and courage, and celebrate moments of triumph and growth along the way.

Identifying Strengths
Start by identifying your strengths, superpowers, and positive qualities. Reflect on moments in your life when you've demonstrated resilience, courage, and determination. These strengths serve as the foundation for your hero narrative, empowering you to confront challenges and overcome adversity.

Navigating Challenges
In your hero narrative, challenges are not seen as insurmountable obstacles but as opportunities for growth and transformation. Approach challenges with a mindset of curiosity and determination, knowing that each obstacle you overcome brings you one step closer to your goals.

Overcoming Adversity
Celebrate moments of triumph and growth along your journey. Recognize the progress you've made, no matter how small, and acknowledge the strength and resilience it took to get there. By reframing adversity as a catalyst for growth, you can cultivate a sense of empowerment and agency in your life.

Embracing Empowerment
Ultimately, changing your narrative from victimhood to heroism is about reclaiming your agency and embracing empowerment. It's about recognizing that you have the power to shape your own story, regardless of the challenges you face. By reframing your narrative, you can cultivate hope, courage, and resilience in the face of addiction's

shadow, empowering yourself to navigate relationships with strength and determination.

In the journey of loving someone with addiction, changing your narrative from victim to hero is a powerful act of empowerment. By recognizing your strengths, confronting challenges with resilience and courage, and celebrating moments of triumph and growth, you can reclaim your agency and cultivate hope for the future. Embrace your role as the hero of your own story, and empower yourself to navigate relationships with strength, resilience, and determination.

Steps For Changing Narrative
Narrative Changing: Changing your narrative involves reframing the way you perceive and interpret your life experiences, particularly challenging ones, in a way that empowers and uplifts you. Here's an example:

Original Narrative: "I'm always the victim in my relationships. I attract partners who mistreat me, and I never seem to find happiness."

Reframed Narrative: "I've faced challenges in my relationships, but I've learned valuable lessons from each experience. I'm resilient and capable of setting boundaries that honor my worth. I'm on a journey of self-discovery and growth, and each relationship teaches me more about what I truly desire and deserve."

In this example, we shift from seeing ourselves as a perpetual victim to recognizing their resilience and capacity for growth. They acknowledge their past challenges but frame them as opportunities for learning and self-discovery. This reframed narrative empowers them to take control of their relationships and create a more positive and fulfilling future.

 **Narrative Changing Exercise**

To change your narrative, you can
Identify Patterns: Recognize recurring themes or beliefs in your current narrative that may be holding you back or causing distress.

Challenge Assumptions: Question the accuracy and validity of your current narrative. Are there alternative interpretations or perspectives that could be more empowering?

Focus on Strengths: Highlight your strengths, accomplishments, and moments of resilience. Acknowledge the ways in which you've overcome challenges in the past.

Set Positive Intentions: Define how you want your narrative to change and set intentions for the future. What kind of story do you want to tell about yourself?

Practice Self-Compassion: Be gentle with yourself as you work to change your narrative. It's okay to acknowledge past struggles, but also remember to celebrate your progress and growth.

By consciously reframing your narrative in a more empowering light, you can cultivate a sense of agency, resilience, and hope for the future.

Reflection: *Reflecting on your past experiences, what narrative have you found yourself repeating that aligns more with feeling like a victim? How would you rewrite this narrative to empower yourself, considering the principles discussed here?*

Embracing Hope: Finding Light in the Darkness of Addiction

How do we define hope when navigating relationships impacted by addiction? Is it placing expectations on others, or finding resilience within ourselves despite challenges? Let's finish the book by delving into the transformative power of hope while in the darkness of addiction's shadow, emphasizing the importance of cultivating optimism and belief in a better future.

In the context of relationships affected by addiction, hope serves as a beacon of strength and resilience amidst adversity. Yet, hope is not merely wishful thinking or relying on others for happiness; it's about cultivating optimism and belief in our ability to create positive change, regardless of external circumstances.

Renowned psychologist Dan Tomasulo introduces the concept of learned hopefulness, emphasizing the importance of nurturing a mindset that recognizes hope as a learned skill. This entails actively seeking reasons for optimism, focusing on positive outcomes, and embracing our capacity to overcome challenges and shape our future.

Hope uplifts us, inspiring resilience, courage, and determination in the face of uncertainty. It's a gift we give ourselves, daring to envision a better tomorrow and holding onto that vision amidst overwhelming circumstances. Hope empowers us to focus on our well-being and growth, independent of whether our partner chooses recovery.

Ultimately, hope is about trusting in our resilience and capacity to navigate challenges, embracing the belief that we can find meaning and happiness amidst difficulties. It's not about relying on others to fix our problems, but about recognizing our own agency and taking proactive steps towards creating the life we desire. In the darkness of addiction's shadow, hope illuminates the path forward, guiding us towards a future filled with possibility, purpose, and fulfillment.

In what ways do you believe cultivating hope can positively influence your outlook on the future and empower you to move forward with resilience and determination, especially in the midst of challenging circumstances like loving someone with addiction?

In the journey of loving someone with addiction, changing our narrative from victim to hero is a transformative act of empowerment. By recognizing our strengths, confronting challenges with resilience, and celebrating moments of growth, we can cultivate hope for the future. As we embrace our role as the hero of our own story, we empower ourselves to navigate relationships with determination and courage. Let hope be our guiding light in the darkness of addiction's shadow, illuminating the path forward towards a future filled with possibility and fulfillment.

To Summarize

As we reflect on the key insights gained from navigating relationships affected by addiction, we are reminded of the paramount importance of self-care. Prioritizing our well-being is not just a luxury but a necessity, providing us with the resilience and clarity needed to make decisions aligned with our values. Moreover, courage emerges as the cornerstone of growth and transformation, empowering us to embrace vulnerability and pursue authenticity in our relationships. By fostering courageous connections within a supportive community, we find solace and strength in knowing that we are not alone in our journey. Finally, hope shines through the darkness, not as a reliance on external circumstances, but as a steadfast belief in the possibility of a brighter future, regardless of the choices our loved ones make. Together, these insights offer guidance and encouragement as we navigate the complexities of loving someone with addiction, reminding us to nurture ourselves, cultivate courage, seek support, and hold onto hope in the face of adversity.

Key Insights:

Prioritizing Self-Care in Tough Relationships: When loving someone with addiction, self-care is vital. It's more than just surface-level activities; it's about nurturing your physical, emotional, and mental well-being. By investing in self-care, you build resilience and clarity, empowering yourself to make decisions that honor your values and promote your overall well-being.

Finding Your Courage: Despite the challenges posed by relationships affected by addiction, cultivating courage and clarity in envisioning a future filled with hope and possibility is essential. By embracing the transformative power of visualization and goal-setting, individuals can navigate relationship complexities with resilience and determination, empowering themselves to take proactive steps towards their dreams and aspirations.

Courageous Connections: While it's natural to feel isolated, reaching out to others who understand your experiences can provide immense comfort and strength. You are not alone—there is a community waiting to welcome you with open arms and walk alongside you every step of the way.

Empowering Narratives and Embracing Hope Amidst Addiction's Shadow: Despite the challenges of loving someone with addiction, hope transcends external circumstances and empowers us to envision a future filled with possibility and resilience. By embracing empowering narratives, we reclaim our agency and navigate relationships with strength and resilience, becoming the heroes of our own stories.

Consolidating Our Insights: Affirming our value and prioritizing self-care are foundational for making tough relationship decisions, especially in relationships affected by addiction. When we recognize our worth and prioritize our well-being, we empower ourselves to make choices that honor our needs and values.

Courage is essential for navigating difficult decisions, and crafting a vision for our future can provide clarity and direction. By envisioning the life we want to create, we gain the courage to take steps towards that vision, whether it involves staying in the relationship or leaving.

Embracing community can offer invaluable support and guidance during challenging times. Connecting with others who understand our experiences can provide comfort and perspective, helping us make informed decisions that align with our values and goals.

Hope is a powerful force that can sustain us through difficult times. Believing in the possibility of a better future, whether in the context of our relationships or our personal growth, can inspire us to persevere and take positive action.

Ultimately, this journey of self-discovery and empowerment supports us in navigating tough relationship decisions touched by addiction by offering us love and support along the way. Through self-awareness and clarity, we can make decisions that honor our well-being and lead to greater fulfillment in our relationships.

> **Reflection:** *Reflecting on our journey, how has affirming your own value and prioritizing self-care influenced your approach to navigating relationships touched by addiction? Consider the role courage has played. How has crafting a vision for your future given you the courage to take steps towards that vision, even amidst uncertainty? Reflect on the power of hope. How has believing in the possibility of a better future inspired you to persevere and take positive action?*

CONCLUSION
TAINTED LOVE

Finding Light in the Shadows of Addiction

My heartfelt wish for you as you continue on your path is to find peace amidst the challenges, strength in moments of doubt, and clarity in times of confusion. May you embrace your journey with courage and resilience, knowing that every step forward is a testament to your growth and inner wisdom. Trust in your ability to navigate life's twists and turns, and may you always be guided by the light of hope and the warmth of love.

The challenge to navigate the complexities of tainted love, whether it's choosing to stay, go, or find a middle ground, is a deeply personal journey. Throughout this book, my aim has been to empower you with self-awareness, knowledge about addiction, and the realization that what you're experiencing is shared by many others facing similar challenges. I hope you've gained valuable tools of resilience and inner strength, as well as clarity or the empowerment to prioritize yourself.

If you're looking for additional resources to reclaim your power and continue your journey towards resilience, self-care, and self-compassion, I invite you to explore my other books: "***Saving You Is Killing Me: Loving Someone with an Addiction***," which offers compassionate support as you reclaim your power and utilizes positive psychology to build resilience; and "***Saving Me One Day at a Time: Finding Light***

Amidst the Shadows of Addiction," providing daily support along your journey. If you have children at home, I also have a children's book titled "***Sunshine Through The Clouds,***" which offers a gentle and supportive exploration of hope and resilience for young readers.

Reflecting on Our Journey

Just by acknowledging the challenges we have both faced together, I hope you feel a sense of connection and understanding. May you have discovered insights and gone on self-discoveries that will guide you on your personal journey. Remember to give yourself grace—allowing yourself to embrace imperfection, forgiveness, and kindness towards yourself and others. The journey of navigating addiction is not an easy one.

I named the book "Tainted Love: Stay or Go? Navigating Tough Relationship Decisions in Addiction" to encapsulate the profound complexities of loving someone battling addiction. "Tainted love" signifies a relationship that has been compromised or destroyed by external influences, particularly addiction, which can erode trust, intimacy, and happiness.

Through this title, I aimed to capture the essence of the book, which delves into the challenging decisions individuals face when loving someone with addiction. I wanted to convey the emotional turmoil, the questioning of whether to stay or leave, and the struggle to find clarity amidst the chaos.

Throughout the book, my goal was to provide you, the readers, with a compassionate and empowering exploration of enlightenment and self-discovery. By sharing insights, tools, and personal messages, I hoped to guide you on a transformative journey towards understanding yourself, your relationships, and the impact of addiction.

Ultimately, I envisioned the book as a beacon of hope and resilience, offering readers the courage to embrace their own growth, reclaim their hearts, and navigate their paths with clarity and empowerment. My aspiration was for "Tainted Love" to be more than just a book—it's a companion for those facing tough relationship decisions, providing support, guidance, and inspiration along the way.

Expressing Gratitude

I want to express my heartfelt gratitude for trusting me as your guide on this journey. It was clear to me from the beginning that remaining neutral was paramount, recognizing that each individual's journey is unique and deeply personal. What may be the right decision for one person could be entirely different for another. I understood that my role was to provide guidance and a framework for empowerment and enlightenment, allowing readers to make informed decisions while safeguarding their mental health throughout the process.

In a world where advice often comes with a heavy dose of judgment or lacks understanding of the complexities of addiction, I aimed to offer readers a different approach. Rather than prescribing solutions or passing judgment, I encouraged self-exploration and reflection. I wanted readers to feel supported in their journey, free from judgment and pressure, so they could navigate their path with clarity, confidence, and compassion for themselves and their loved ones.

I am deeply grateful for your trust and commitment throughout this journey. Thank you for allowing me to accompany you through this challenging situation. Your strength and vulnerability have been truly inspiring, and I am honored to have been a part of your process.

My Final Note Dear Reader,

As we come to the end of this journey together, I want to take a moment to remind you of something important: You matter. Your happiness matters. And you are here for a reason—to live a life that is rich with inspiration and joy. Hold onto this truth tightly as you move forward, knowing deep within your heart that you are deserving of all the love, fulfillment, and peace that life has to offer.

As you go on the next chapter of your journey, please remember this: You've got this. Whatever path you choose to walk, know that you possess the strength, resilience, and inner wisdom needed to navigate it with grace and courage. Embrace the healing process, honor your truth, and continue to seek growth and fulfillment along the way. Always remember that you are supported, and that you are more than capable of creating a life that is filled with purpose and joy.

With so much love and warm hugs,

Andrea Seydel

ABOUT S.Y.K.M. COMMUNITY

Dear Friends and Supporters,

At S.Y.K.M. (Saving You Is Killing Me), our mission is to provide compassionate support and valuable resources to those who love someone struggling with addiction. However, we can't achieve this mission alone. We need your help in spreading the word and extending our reach to individuals and communities in need.

Here are a few ways you can help:

Share our resources with support groups: If you're part of a support group for families or individuals affected by addiction, please consider sharing information about S.Y.K.M. books, podcasts, and the community. Our materials offer insights, understanding, and practical guidance for navigating the challenges of loving someone with addiction. By sharing your thoughts and experiences, you contribute to a community of individuals seeking guidance and inspiration on their own paths to resilience and hope amidst addiction's challenges. Your words may resonate deeply with someone in need of support and understanding.

Inform treatment centers and psychologists: Reach out to local treatment centers and mental health professionals to introduce them to S.Y.K.M. resources. These professionals play a vital role in supporting individuals in recovery, and our materials can offer valuable support to their client's loved ones.

Spread the word through word-of-mouth: Tell your friends, family, and colleagues about S.Y.K.M.. Share your personal experiences with our books, podcasts, and community, and encourage others to explore the resources we offer. Your sharing serves as a gift to others, guiding them toward the inspiration and empowerment found within the pages and community of *"Saving You Is Killing Me."*

Thank you for your support in spreading the message of resilience and love.

Make a donation: As a volunteer-based organization, every contribution makes a difference in our ability to continue providing support and resources to those in need. Your donation helps us maintain our website, produce podcasts, and create new materials to support families affected by addiction.

Advocate for inclusive support: Highlight the importance of supporting loved ones of individuals struggling with addiction. While there is significant support available for those in recovery, there remains a gap in support for their families and loved ones. By raising awareness about S.Y.K.M., you're advocating for a more inclusive approach to addiction support—one that doesn't cast shame on those who are affected by their loved one's addiction. Together, we can make a difference in the lives of individuals and families affected by addiction. Thank you for your support and for helping us spread the word about S.Y.K.M..

Leave a Review on Amazon: If the *"Saving You Is Killing Me: Loving Someone with An Addiction"* book series has touched your life, I would be immensely grateful if you could consider leaving an honest review on Amazon or wherever you have purchased this book. Your review holds the power to make a significant difference in helping others discover the transformative journey depicted in this book.

To leave a review on Amazon:
- Visit the book's Amazon page.
- Scroll down to the "Customer Reviews" section.
- Click on the "Write a Customer Review" button.
- Share your honest thoughts and insights about the book.

Explore Our Other Books: Explore our series of books, including "*Saving You Is Killing Me: Loving Someone with An Addiction,*" "*Saving Me One Day at a Time: Finding Light Amidst the Shadows of Addiction,*" "*Tainted Love: A Stay-or-Go Guide to Making Tough Relationship Decisions in the face of Addiction,*" "*Are You Still In There? Understanding Addiction: A Guide for Families and Loved Ones,*" and the children's book "*Sunshine Through The Clouds: A Young Heart's Journey of Resilience Through Family Addiction.*"

Stay Connected:
Resilience in positive psychology is about more than just weathering life's storms—it's about bouncing back stronger and wiser. At S.Y.K.M. (Saving You Is Killing Me), we understand the challenges of loving someone with addiction, and we're here to support you on your journey to resilience and well-being. We're not just a community; we're a family who intimately knows the turmoil of loving someone with addiction. Utilizing the principles of positive psychology and human flourishing, we offer a nurturing environment aimed at enhancing the well-being of our community.

Join our community on social media to stay updated on upcoming events, discussions, and additional resources:

Instagram: @savingyouiskillingme

Facebook Private Group: Saving You Is Killing Me: Loving Someone With An Addiction

Podcast: The Saving You Is Killing Me: Loving Someone with An Addiction Podcast

Youtube: Saving You Is Killing Me: Loving An Addict

Website: www.andreaseydel.com | www.savingyouiskillingme.com

Resources and References:

 Visit our website for references, research, resources, and suggested reading to support your journey to resilience and well-being

Bounce back, regain your power, and build fortitude using positive psychology. We're here for you every step of the way. And lastly, if you're curious about putting yourself first, take our MEFIRST Challenge to reclaim your sparkle

and prioritize your well-being. Through this complimentary resource, you'll have the opportunity to explore what matters most to you, uncover sources of happiness, and identify growth opportunities in your life. Access it here: www.savingyouiskillingme.com

Remember, you're not alone on this journey. Together, we can empower more individuals to find light amidst the shadows of addiction and create lives filled with hope and resilience.

Thank you for being a part of this incredible journey.

Sending Hugs Your Way,

Andrea Seydel

ABOUT THE AUTHOR

Andrea Seydel is a leading expert in the field of positive psychology, holding a degree in psychology with post-graduate training in positive psychology and resilience.

With a deep commitment to helping others, Andrea is the founder of "Saving You is Killing Me: Loving Someone with an Addiction." This multifaceted initiative includes a vibrant community, an enlightening podcast, and a series of books dedicated to supporting those who love individuals struggling with addiction.

Beyond her academic qualifications, Andrea has personally navigated the painful journey of loving and losing someone to addiction, giving her a profound understanding of the challenges faced by families in such situations.

Her insights into resilience and human flourishing are grounded in both her professional expertise and her lived experiences.

A regular contributor to "Recovery Today" magazine, Andrea is a passionate advocate for those who find themselves in the shadows of addiction. Her dedication to providing support, guidance, and hope to individuals and families impacted by addiction shines through in her work.

For more information and to connect with Andrea please visit andrea-seydel.com or reach out to her directly at savingyouiskillingme.com.

Andrea Seydel is committed to helping others find light, strength, and resilience in the face of addiction's challenges.

ABOUT THE PUBLISHER

Dear Reader,

As you hold this remarkable book in your hands, we want to express our heartfelt gratitude for becoming a part of the Live Life Happy Community of readers. Your curiosity and thirst for knowledge fuel our passion for publishing meaningful non-fiction works.

At Live Life Happy Publishing, our mission is rooted in bringing forth literature that not only entertains but uplifts, supports, and nourishes the soul. We firmly believe that books have the power to transform lives, to ignite passions, and to spread joy far and wide.

Behind every word, every chapter, lies the dedication of our authors who pour their hearts and souls into their craft. Their ultimate aim? To touch your life in profound ways, to inspire, and to leave an indelible mark on your journey.

Your role in this journey is invaluable; by sharing your thoughts through reviews, spreading the word to others, or reaching out to the authors themselves, you become an integral part of sparking transformation in countless lives, igniting a ripple effect of joy and enlightenment.

And if, perchance, you or someone you know has dreams of writing, of sharing a message, or of unleashing a powerful story unto the world, know that Live Life Happy Publishing stands ready to guide you. Our doors are open, our ears attuned, and our hearts eager to hear your message.

So, dear reader, let us, continue to spread the power of literature, one page at a time. Reach out, share, and most importantly, never underestimate the power of your message to touch lives.

With warmest regards,

LiveLifeHappyPublishing.com

P.S. Remember, books change lives. Whose life will you touch with yours?

www.ingramcontent.com/pod-product-compliance
Lightning Source LLC
Chambersburg PA
CBHW070550160426
43199CB00014B/2450